T0340223

The Impacts of Neoliberalism on US Community Colleges

Focusing on community colleges as a unique structure within American higher education, this text investigates the specific ways in which these institutions have been impacted by a global increase in neoliberal education policies.

Analyzing the effects neoliberalism has had on community colleges, the text charters discourse relating the erosion of faculty voice in academic governance, and decision making; the vocationalization of curriculum; and the impact that these factors have had on the ability of community colleges to provide students with an education that supports a democratic society. Exposing a movement away from the historical aims of community-based education, the text evidences a hijacking of community colleges to serve the objectives of the corporate elite. There has been a decline in community college faculty engagement in shared governance and their loss of recognition as academic and curricular leaders, and the book discusses the potential for redistribution of decision-making power back toward faculty.

This text will be of great interest to graduate and postgraduate students, academics, professionals and policy-makers in the fields of Higher Education, Education Policy and Politics, Sociology of Education, Higher Education Management and Education Politics.

Greg Sethares is Professor of Mathematics at Bristol Community College, Massachusetts, US.

Routledge Studies in Education, Neoliberalism, and Marxism

Series editor Dave Hill, Anglia Ruskin University, Chelmsford and Cambridge, England

For more information about this series, please visit: https://www.routledge.com/

The Impacts of Neoliberalism on US Community Colleges
Reclaiming Faculty Voice in Academic Governance

Greg Sethares

Routledge
Taylor & Francis Group

NEW YORK AND LONDON

First published 2020
by Routledge
52 Vanderbilt Avenue, New York, NY 10017

and by Routledge
2 Park Square, Milton Park, Abingdon, Oxon, OX14 4RN

Routledge is an imprint of the Taylor & Francis Group, an informa business

© 2020 Taylor & Francis

Library of Congress Cataloging-in-Publication Data
A catalog record for this title has been requested

ISBN: 978-0-367-86045-5 (hbk)
ISBN: 978-0-367-49725-5 (pbk)
ISBN: 978-1-003-01664-9 (ebk)

Typeset in Times New Roman
by codeMantra

For my wife and best friend, Kris, whose love and support made this book, and all worthwhile things in my life, possible. I love you.

For our daughters, Kaitlyn and Jillian, with whom I shared an educational journey during this project. Your love of learning and kindness toward others always inspires me.

Contents

Preface

The research which led to this book is grounded in consideration of the impact neoliberal ideology, a proposition that all of human existence can best be served through individual responsibility and free market entrepreneurialism, has had on education policy over the past four decades, specifically as related to community colleges. My work includes analyses of seminal works by leading critical intellectuals both within and beyond the field of education and the Western epistemological platform, including Agamben, Fraser, Freire, Giroux, Harvey, Lefebvre, Sousa Santos, and others. This qualitative study consists of purely textual analysis, and my own perspective is, of course, an integral component of the research process. In this introduction, I situate the project and circumstances which led to the writing of the book, and more explicitly describe the study itself.

Qualitative research is concerned with the interaction of the object of study with the surrounding social environment. It engages in critical dialog about how the object interacts with issues such as race, gender, class, globalization, and democracy. My work is no different; I locate my object of study in a deeply social context, one in which I have been engaged for many years, as I strive to connect my work "to the hopes, needs, goals, and promises of a free democratic society" (Denzin & Lincoln, 2000, p. 3). This book, with its evaluations and conclusions, is not intended to provide a roadmap or a common recipe for success, but is instead a public statement of the results of my analysis.

The trajectory of every qualitative study is unique, being formed, deformed, and re-formed by the context in which the researcher performs the study. This context may be quite varied, and may include the personal experiences and biases of the researcher. In this regard, I am no different, as I bring to this study a variety of experiences and biases that do not put me in one easy-to-interpret position. I have had a long career as an educator, faculty member, union officer, advocate for faculty involvement in academic decision-making, and senior administrator. While some may regard my employment history as a strength, others may view it as a limitation. I have recognized my own biases during the research process as both a faculty member and an administrator, and these sometimes-conflicting positions have made me aware of certain challenges, ethical procedures, and limits in both perspectives. I am now more aware and cautious about ethical boundaries that can be easily but dangerously transcended.

Other limiting factors of this study stem from my own experiences, biases, beliefs, and preferences. My textual analysis has been based on works written by leading critical social theorists and philosophers whom I selected. Why did I focus on one theorist or philosopher over another? Why one work over another by the same author? Did I openly consider literature that contradicted my biases and beliefs? These questions reflect how the qualitative researcher is situated within their research, analysis, and interpretation. I do not take this as a negative aspect of the study but as an inherent limitation of any qualitative research done by an individual with a lifetime of lived experiences, beliefs, and values. Given my particular focus and the choices I made during this project, along with my own particular experiences and circumstances, this book may hold some limitations for those who wish to broadly generalize its findings. The reader thus must understand this book as one person's interpretation of social environment. While the analysis and interpretation presented in this book may or may not be suited for application to all such circumstances, it may nonetheless motivate others and serve as a starting point from which readers may be moved to ask more questions, critique other social environments, and find solutions for their particular situations, institutions, and communities.

As I have undertaken this qualitative research and have engaged the object of my study, I have done so with a conspicuously present life history. This history includes personal and professional life experiences that have influenced the person I am and led me to this particular project, which draws heavily on those experiences. Thus, my personal history has no doubt had a profound impact on my analysis and interpretations. I also have addressed the object of my study through textual analyses of the writings of leading critical theorists. As I am unable to separate my life experiences from my analysis and interpretations based on these writings, my research has evolved into a deeply personal study.

In conducting my analysis, I have attempted to move the most dominant and hegemonic social and political forces to the margins in order to create a space of dialog and public debate, one that can be claimed by those who may have been silenced. I do not pretend to speak for those silenced voices, but I do strive to create an opportunity for discourse, and provide a platform and climate for them, and for their analyses and interpretations. In this process, I have attempted to serve as a *parrhesiastes*—from the ancient Greek concept of *parrhesia*—one who speaks with frankness and "opens his heart and mind completely to other people through his discourse . . . avoiding any kind of rhetorical form which would veil what he thinks" (Foucault & Pearson, 2001, p. 12). In parrhesia, "there is always an exact coincidence between belief and truth." One who truly engages in parrhesia "says what he *knows* to be true," but such knowledge does not require the modern Cartesian conception of evidence to be proven true (Foucault & Pearson, 2001, p. 14). Parrhesia is thus inconsistent with the current-day conception of knowledge, which freely engages in rhetorical and technical forms of argument and proof. While my analysis and interpretation do rely on modern statements of evidential proof, I also claim as a foundation of my work— specifically as it relates to my life experiences—my ability and the ability of all others who continue this dialog to engage in parrhesia. The parrhesiastes who completely open heart and mind to others also open themselves to criticism and risk their status in modern society. However, taking such risks also opens up the opportunity and ability to engage in genuine critique and to speak their truth as their duty to society (Foucault & Pearson, 2001). The unique experience of such individuals cannot be overemphasized, as it makes it impossible for anyone to undermine their intellectual understanding.

My own life experiences and resultant biases have driven me to this place and to this study. They have framed the way I see the social and political worlds around me, including the relationships between individuals and their environs, personal relationships, opportunities for happiness, renewal, and intellectual stimulation. They have influenced the value system that has guided my life view. As I situate myself within this study and within my own text as both interpretive and political bricoleur, I am fully aware that my research is heavily value-laden. As I engage in this deeply social research study, I acknowledge the intensely personal and social elements of my own life, vis-à-vis both my personal life history and a long professional history in the vocation of education—which may be seen as one of the most profoundly political and social sciences.

Making decisions in a higher education institution involves a variety of interrelated subject and work areas, making it a necessarily participatory process. These decisions may include determining institutional investment strategy, managing the physical plant, setting budget priorities, making human resources decisions, determining programmatic offerings, and setting academic policies. Many involve academic issues or tangentially impact academic matters; thus, there often is an assumption that faculty are—or should be—involved in such decisions. Who is and is not involved in making such decisions is vitally important, as educational decisions are by nature political and making them constitutes a political act (Apple, 1979).

When faculty are engaged (to varying extent) in the decision-making process, it is often referred to as "shared governance." There is no generally accepted definition of shared governance, as the wide variety of governance models in higher education inherently reflects specific institutional circumstances and ideological positions. Given the current neoliberal political context, the term is often an empty and floating signifier (Laclau, 2005) that has been appropriated by different constituencies. Jenkins and Jensen (2010) state that true shared governance can only occur when those impacted by a decision have a say in making it and, in the case of education, when administrators defer to faculty on academic matters. Tinberg et al. (2009) profess not only that decision-makers must value faculty input, but also that faculty must educate themselves in the workings of their institution and understand the administrative pressures decision-makers face. With no commonly accepted definition, what constitutes shared governance is continually being discussed and debated. This book will avoid the task of determining whether shared governance does or does not exist in a particular situation. It will focus instead on the extent to which faculty are and have been engaged in decision-making at their institutions, as well as the impact of their engagement in the process—past, present, and potential.

With the increased prominence of US community colleges, and the notable growth in the proportion of US college students attending community colleges and receiving an education that has become increasingly focused on middle-skilled employment—that is, employment requiring more than a high school diploma but less than a baccalaureate degree (Levin, Kater, & Wagoner, 2006)—more analysis is needed. Such analysis is important not only for those students but for the future of the democratic society they will support. In this rapidly and dramatically changing educational environment, a study and reevaluation of faculty voice in academic matters is of critical import, as it will allow consideration of political and economic alternatives for students beyond narrowly defined economic limits. This book will illustrate that authentic faculty involvement in governance can help guide community colleges in a direction that will "keep alive the promise of eliminating the current cohabitation of low-intensity democracy and economic despotism" (Sousa Santos, 2014, p. 181). It will show that faculty have the power to guide institutions away from being mechanisms of corporate-driven, middle-skilled employment training and toward being institutions that provide students with the skills needed to succeed in the workforce, as well as the skills of citizenship that support democratic structures in our society. This book will show that authentic faculty participation—that is, participation not orchestrated by institutional efforts to control (Anderson, 1998)—can lead to a future in which community colleges lead the way not only to a better life for their students but to a more authentic society of praxis.

Vitally important to this work are the characteristics of community college students. More than in other segments of higher education, community colleges educate urban students, first-generation college students, and students marginalized by factors such as race, ethnicity, class, gender, and varying abilities and disabilities. To connect the impact of a community college education to the creation of a more authentic society demands consideration of community college students and their ability to impact the communities in which they live. For urban neighborhoods dominated by gentrification, poverty, and problems related to housing, food, and social insecurity, a community college education is a vital—and in many cases the only—avenue to an education that fosters the skills and attributes present and future urban leaders will need to claim and reclaim the conditions of their existence, and, in so doing, to generate a more authentic society based on a democratic platform. While the fundamental focus of this study is community college faculty governance, the impact of such governance on institutional curricula and the students who benefit from such an education is a critical motivating factor.

Research regarding faculty governance in higher education has to some degree been dominated by research on the university. While community colleges are an ever more significant part of the higher education landscape, in relative terms they are far less frequently explored than the university. For example, a preliminary search of the Google Scholar database using the descriptor "community college faculty governance" yielded 221,000 entries, while the descriptor "university faculty governance" yielded 1,440,000—more than six times the number of entries. Using the descriptor "university shared governance" yielded almost three and one-half times the number of entries than the descriptor "community college shared governance." When comparing "university faculty voice" to "community college faculty voice," the former outnumbered the latter almost three to one. This book has the potential to add to the more limited body of knowledge and scholarship on community colleges in the current neoliberal environment.

The shared experiences of community college educators are examined throughout this work. Fundamental to their condition is the lack of faculty oversight of academic matters and the hegemonic control imposed by market-driven forces. Control over the curriculum, which historically has been in the hands of faculty, has been eroded. Regaining faculty voice and returning institutional and system-wide curricular decisions to academic rather than market interests holds promise as a strategy for renewal of the entire community college system.

While many may not recognize the oppressed subculture within higher education that consists not only of community college students but of community college educators, the community college system in the United States has been used and shaped to serve market desire. While this use is not unique to community colleges, as universities have experienced a similar transformation (H. A. Giroux, 2014a), the extent to which community colleges have been singled out as centers of vocational training is unique within higher education. To get beyond this, educators at these institutions must regain their collective voice. To be truly revolutionary, this voice must include those who have been oppressed (Freire, 2000) and must be heard in a space where testimony and genuine dialog are not only allowed but expected and welcomed. Such a "space of healing and empowerment" (Espino, Vega, Rendón, Ranero, & Muniz, 2012) must be created carefully and deliberately, and all must be invited to participate in the dialog. This space must be occupied by the oppressed, even if they do not yet understand that they have been oppressed, thus giving the entire community a locus of empowerment and transformation.

In this book, I strive to create a space in which one may examine the erosion and in some cases the complete absence of faculty voice in academic decision-making since the emergence of neoliberal education policies over the past four decades. My analysis focusses on the role of faculty and the power of their voices. Much has been written about the impact of neoliberalism within the university, and I build on this body of knowledge by situating my study in US community colleges. The specific focus will be on investigating and understanding the relationship between community college faculty and the process of making academic decisions.

I examine the primary tenets of the neoliberal ideological framework, including how the managerial state promulgated by neoliberal theory has colonized higher education faculty by reducing the importance of their participation in issues related to governance, and in academic and institutional decision-making. In so doing, I investigate the associated implications within the new political economy of higher education. I then frame the major community college reforms of the past four decades within the cultural context of neoliberalism and its hegemonic impact on community college education policy, and scrutinize how such policies should be understood within the complex political economy of education systems. I also investigate the critical role community colleges play in educating urban populations, using the lens of Lefebvre's (1996) "right to the city" concept to connect the conditions of community college education to the educational attributes urban students need to remake the conditions of their daily existence. Finally, I claim the role community college faculty should play in academic decision-making as a matter of recognition and redistribution (Fraser, 2000), and as a way to promote a more just and democratic society through educational processes based in an ecology of knowledges (Sousa Santos, 2014).

The book examines the erosion of faculty voice in academic decision-making over the last forty years. This framework navigates five major terrains: (a) the tenets of neoliberal ideology; (b) the impact of neoliberal policies on higher education faculty participation in institutional decision-making; (c) four decades of community college reforms framed within the matrix of neoliberal policies; (d) Lefebvre's (1996) concept of right to the city, which is crucial to understanding the circumstances and needs of urban community college students; and (e) faculty engagement as a matter of recognition and redistribution.

To examine the metamorphoses of these terrains, I will rely on approaches edified by leading critical intellectuals and educators from within and beyond the field of education and Western epistemological platforms. In this context, approaches designed by Aronowitz, Dewey, Fraser, Giroux, Harvey, Lipman, Veblen, and others will allow me not only to address the primary focus of the book—that is, exploring the ways in which the engagement and influence of faculty in academic decision-making has diminished over four decades of neoliberal education policies—but also to recognize the consequences of that erosion. These approaches cannot be understood as monolithic. In fact, in the analysis I strive to expose myself, the study, and the reader to multiple contrasting epistemological avenues within the same ideological disposition. While I draw from a specific epistemological position, I am aware of the complex epistemological matrix with which I am engaged, working within areas such as philosophy, political science, sociology, and decolonial theories.

This framework allows what for me has been a deep and personal study that also seeks to address broader questions:

• What impact has the loss of community college faculty voice in academic and institutional governance had on the curriculum and purpose of these institutions?
• How may we redress the current circumstances regarding loss of community college faculty voice?

The framework of this book has been designed to lead the study and the reader through a series of smaller conversations, including a study of factors contributing to the current state of affairs in higher education, examining both the loss of voice of university faculty in recent decades and the less-traveled terrain of the loss of voice of community college faculty. The framework will also allow us to consider the importance of these changes in terms of students' democratic and social lives and leadership in their communities. The study specifically investigates the connections between curricula and the skills and attributes urban community college students need to develop into community leaders and claim their right to define the conditions of their own existence.

This introduction is followed by six chapters, organized within the framework described above, that will guide the study and the reader through a complex historical, social, and political milieu of interrelated considerations, both public and private. Chapter 1 includes a study of the primary tenets of neoliberalism, an analysis of the post-World War II social welfare state, and its contradictions with and ultimate demise at the hands of neoliberal policy.

Consideration is given to economic, social, and historical factors that provided sustenance for the development and installation of neoliberal ideology throughout the world. The chapter concludes with a discussion of the current status of neoliberal policies and practices as a globally dominant philosophy. Chapter 2 examines the history of shared governance in US universities, including the major circumstances related to its rise to prominence and its precipitous decline over the past four decades. The interrogation contemplates not only the role of faculty in the university but the economic, social, and democratic purpose of the university. In Chapter 3, the discussion of the university is extended to the American community college, including its history and adaptable mission. This includes a focus on the increased alignment of these institutions with providing education and workforce training which are supported by both state and corporate interests and closely associated with an increasing vocationalization of the community college curriculum. Also considered is the population of US residents most likely to attend a community college and thus to encounter such workforce training and vocation-oriented curriculum. This calls for a critical examination of whether these factors also point to a subalternization of the community college student, providing a different educational experience to some students based on the type of higher education afforded them by their life circumstances.

Chapter 4 considers the impact the urban community college has and has had on society using Lefebvre's (1996) notion of the right to the city, which examines urban residents' ability to define the conditions of their own daily existence. Discriminating between the specific technical skills for employment that may be taught within a vocationalized curriculum and the social and political leadership skills often associated with a liberal arts education, the analysis will scrutinize the role urban community colleges play in providing an education that supports their students' ability to claim their right to the city. The chapter also includes further examination of the importance of community college faculty members' role in matters related to shared governance, specifically as related to curriculum. Chapter 5 extends the analysis of community college faculty engagement in shared governance with a consideration of Fraser's (2000) notion of recognition and redistribution. The argument is made that recognition of community college faculty should not mimic recognition of a group-specific identity, but that each faculty member should be recognized as a full and valued member of the institutional governance process. It will be argued that faculty may reclaim curriculum control from state and corporate influence, thereby wresting epistemic privilege, exemplified by a vocational-ized education with an emphasis on the specific and technical skills for middle-skilled employment, away from neoliberal authority and paving the way for an education designed to support students' right to the city.

Finally, in the Conclusion, I offer some culminating thoughts based on the discussions within the varied terrains traversed in the book. In this process, recognizing that the writing of this book is the conclusion of a deeply social, political, and personal study, I have situated myself within the study and this text as an interpre-tive and political *bricoleur* who has relied on textual analysis of the writings of leading critical intellectuals. In this process, it cannot be ignored that my own personal and professional life experiences have been present, as I have crafted an interpretation which for me has deep personal meaning. The framework described in the five interconnected chapters which follow led me to this interpre-tation and conclusion. It is my sincere hope that my own interpre-tations and conclusions will not be an end, but will prompt further dialog and consideration for the reader.

With this in mind, and with an eye toward situating developments in the educational realm, I open the framework of this study with an examination of the primary tenets of neoliberal ideology. I examine the post-World War II social welfare state and the conversion nar-rative that has guided its demise over the past four decades, along with its move toward a dominant commonsense ethic that values market exchange and individual rights and freedoms. Analysis will include the role of the state, the consequential conflict between the theory and practice of neoliberalism, the use of the instrument of debt, and the confused distinction between financialization and the fabric of human existence.

Acknowledgments

The journey which led to the writing of this book would not have been possible without the example and inspiration of my parents, Anita and George Sethares. My mother welcomed me into her life engaged in peace and social justice activism, teaching me at the youngest of ages that the world was much larger than the small town in which we lived, and that our actions mattered to others and to the world. My father shared with me his life engaged in academic, intellectual, and naturalist pursuits. Whether walking in the woods or weeding the garden, my time with my father has always been connected to learning about people and the natural world. My parents inspired and instructed me through the shared experiences of lives engaged in intellectual, social, environmental, and political pursuits. Without their example of critical reflection and activism, I would not be the person I am, nor would I have ever engaged in the journey which led to this book.

I am deeply indebted to Joao Paraskeva for his friendship, guidance, and dedication to social and epistemological justice. Selfless with his time and critique, Joao swayed me to consider domains that were previously unknown to me, and which ultimately played vital roles in the foundation of this study. I am grateful for the expertise, advice, and support of Jennifer Elizabeth Brunton. I am grateful not only for her insightful critique but for her story, and the inspiration and encouragement she provided me to finish the project. I am thankful to Ken Saltman for introducing me to research regarding the many calculated forces negatively impacting urban education in the United States, research which introduced me to Lefebvre's notion of Right to the City, which had a significant impact on the framework of this book. I owe thanks to Ricardo Rosa who has influenced the way I consider forces of power and how they impact public policy, a perspective critical to this book and the way I see the world. I am indebted to Donaldo Macedo, for the friendship, support, and inspiration he provided to me and other members of my cohort in the Educational Leadership and Policy Studies Program at the University of Massachusetts Dartmouth. Selflessly offering his time to support the research of others, Donaldo is an inspiration to me and a significant force in support of claiming one's voice, and naming the world. To my Educational Leadership and Policy Studies cohort members, I express my gratitude, admiration, and friendship. Your passion for social justice continues to motivate me. I am also greatly appreciative of the institutional support during this project provided to me by the University of Massachusetts Dartmouth.

I am grateful to Jack Sbrega for the trust he placed in me, and for the persistent appreciation he showed for my efforts and the efforts of my team. Through his trust and support, I was afforded the opportunity to learn, grow, and discover new abilities, many of which greatly assisted me in completing this project. Thank you, Jack. During the time I wrote this book, I had the distinct honor to serve with a number of academic administrators at Bristol Community College who recognized and valued the crucial role faculty play in academic decision-making. To Anthony, Ana, Ulli, Kathleen, Bill, Lynne, Pat, Sarmad, Meghan, Rodney, April, Bob, and Deb, thank you for your decency, humor, and kindness. You contributed to shaping an administration which respected and valued the essential role of the faculty-administrator. While such times can be fleeting, the space which you helped create serves as a vision of hope and possibility. I am deeply indebted to my faculty and professional staff colleagues at Bristol Community College, particularly to those who have steadfastly supported the Bristol Chapter of the Massachusetts Community College Council, and the college's Faculty and Professional Staff Senate. Through our many years working together, you have repeatedly claimed your voice, and exercised your right to speak your word. Your efforts working on behalf of faculty rights, in order to provide for our students a liberating education, one worthy of their hopes and ideals, is not only laudable, but it is crucial to the futures of our students, and their families and communities.

1 Neoliberalism as a Dominant Ideology

In this chapter I introduce and define the tenets of neoliberalism, examining its historical roots and following its global implementation over the past four decades. I examine the social and political transformation of most developed Western nations from the once-dominant post-World War II social welfare state to the current state in which neoliberal ideology dominates the practices of the state. I examine elements of the unfettered market ethos of neoliberalism, as well as the managerialism that has accompanied this transformation. I also examine the changing functions and responsibilities of the state and the stultifying role debt plays in the current political economy, both of which are critical to understanding the current hegemony of neoliberal ideology.

An uncountable number of social, political, and public policies and practices, including, as I will show, those of universities and community colleges, have been influenced by the widespread implementation of neoliberal ideology over the past four decades. The ideology has spread to most corners of the globe, dominating public and private discourse, policy, and practice, and serving as a structural framework for change, both global and local. This chapter provides a foundational survey of the tenets of neoliberalism, focusing not just on the ideology but on its history, root causes, and essential elements. The narrative investigates classical and modern theories that impact neoliberal theory, such as the new managerialism and the changing role of the state, use of the state of exception, the debilitating tool of debt, the relationship between the political economy and happiness, and the potentially liberating relationship between language and a world dominated by financialization.

Neoliberalism is in the first instance a theory of political economic practices that proposes that human well-being can best be advanced by liberating individual entrepreneurial

freedoms and skills within an institutional framework characterized by strong private property rights, free markets, and free
trade.

(Harvey, 2005, p. 2)

Neoliberal ideology states that, where markets do not exist or
where "rules are not clearly laid out or where property rights are
hard to define, the state must use its power to impose or invent market systems" (Harvey, 2005, p. 65). It further holds that, beyond
the initial creation of the market, government should not interfere.
Indeed, the theory postulates that government should, to the greatest extent possible, not get involved in free markets because "the
state cannot possibly possess enough information to second-guess
market signals (prices)" and "because powerful interest groups will
inevitably distort and bias state interventions (particularly in democracies) for their own benefit" (Harvey, 2005, p. 2). While in practice not all aspects of neoliberalism have been implemented in their
purely theoretical form, many aspects of the ideology remain the
cornerstones of the public/private policy debate.

Throughout this study, we will see numerous contradictions between theory and practice, such as "free" markets made less free
through the corporate and political influences of the financial elite.
Neoliberalism "calls for privatization of public goods and services,
decreased regulation of trade, loosening of capital and labor con-
trols by the state, and the allowance of foreign direct investment"
(Saltman, 2012, p. 96). For decades, these calls for privatization,
deregulation, and the free flow of capital have been at the forefront
of public policy debates. The call for privatization, for example, has
persistently claimed that government agencies—those entrusted to
defend and serve the public and their interests—cannot be trusted
to oversee public services. According to the neoliberal framework,
"public control over public resources should be shifted out of the
hands of the necessarily bureaucratic state and into the hands
of the necessarily efficient private sector" (Saltman, 2012, p. 96).
This contention has defined an ideological divide as to whether the
public or private sector is best suited to the distribution of public
resources, and as such redefines the very meaning of what it means
to be "public." Neoliberal policies have been presented as an impartial solution to social and economic issues, and as the inevitable
evolution of capitalism (Hursh & Henderson, 2011). Neoliberalism is more than a doctrine or an economic theory; it has come
to be a philosophy which governs the practices of the state. What

has made neoliberalism sovereign is that it has been paired with a dominant—and, so far, irrepressible—political plan of action that promotes individual self-interest over the interests of the public (H. A. Giroux, 2014a). No matter the status of the debate regarding distribution of public resources, one fact is quite clear: for the past four decades, neoliberalism, or at least an incarnation of neoliberalism, has been infused in every corner of global society (Saltman, 2012). This dominant implementation has been supported by the corporate elite, who, by successfully controlling and winning the public debate, have "largely succeeded in marginalizing alternative conceptions" (Hursh & Henderson, 2011, p. 172).

Neoliberalism as a doctrine professes that all enterprises are transactional in nature, and that the ultimate measure of all such transactions is the concept of consumerism—the ethos of that which can be bought and sold (Giroux, 2011). The incorporation of neoliberal ideology into every aspect of social, cultural, and political life has caused significant changes in personal and social frameworks. Neoliberal theory holds that profit-driven free-market exchanges, along with individual choice and entrepreneurial freedom, will fix all the world's inequalities, and that the "social good will be maximized by maximizing the reach and frequency of market transactions . . .[therefore,] it seeks to bring all human action into the domain of the market" (Harvey, 2005, p. 3). Neoliberalism, which employs elements of social Darwinism, has no place and allows no excuses for illness, poverty, or other social ills (Weiner, 2012). It entails an individualistic, anti-public rhetoric that explicitly devalues a socially responsible ethic that promotes the conditions for public responsibility and democratic engagement. It "attempts to undermine all forms of solidarity capable of challenging market-driven values and social relations, promoting the virtues of an unbridled individualism almost pathological in its disdain for community, social responsibility, public values, and the public good" (H. A. Giroux, 2014a, p. 2).

Advocates of neoliberal ideology are found in every social, cultural, and commercial venture, including education, government, and corporate entities. Neoliberalism has become so commonplace worldwide that it has "become hegemonic as a mode of discourse. It has pervasive effects on ways of thought to the point where it has become incorporated into the common-sense way many of us interpret, live in, and understand the world" (Harvey, 2005, p. 3).

Over the past four decades, the increasing dominance of neoliberal ideology in all aspects of human existence has coincided with marked advances in information technology. The maximization of market transactions so central to neoliberalism has increased the importance of these advances in information technology, which have made such transactions both more global and nearly instantaneous. This has allowed a broader and faster expansion of neoliberal practices. Neoliberalism values market exchange as "an ethic in itself, capable of acting as a guide to all human action, and substituting for all previously held ethical beliefs" (Harvey, 2005, p. 3). In this environment, neoliberalism has become hegemonic to the point of changing global, national, institutional, social, and personal ethics.

The Post-World War II Social Welfare State

"Freedom from want" was one of four tenets affirmed by US President Franklin Delano Roosevelt as the foundation of his political vision for the future (Harvey, 2005, p. 183). Roosevelt clearly placed blame for the economic and social problems of the Great Depression on the excessive market freedom of the 1920s. He cautioned against the greed which had led to "excessive profits" and "undue private power" (Harvey, 2005, p. 183). Roosevelt's vision of freedom from want extended the state's responsibilities to include protecting citizens from poverty, hunger, and homelessness. This vision, paired with stronger market regulations, helped set the stage for the post-World War II social welfare state. Postwar reforms included a restructuring of state support and regulation to prevent a recurrence of the conditions that led to the global financial collapse of 1929 and the Great Depression, both of which threatened the capitalist order, as well as protecting against the kind of national rivalries that led to World War II (Harvey, 2005).

In Great Britain, postwar restructuring was seen as a compromise between the forces of capital and labor, of free-market capitalism and an increase in socialist public provisions offered through the state. This entailed a settlement between conflicting free-market and Keynesian principles of economic planning which allowed public spending on social and welfare services. A state administration was called for to implement these services, and to provide a stable, predictable, and socially neutral force for their delivery (Clarke & Newman, 1997). Such an administration was to be both impartial and impersonal, insulating policy from implementation, showing no favoritism, dealing with facts, and making fair and unbiased decisions. It was to be moderated by the influence of professionals such as medical personnel, educators, and social workers, who would work in tandem with the administration. Medical personnel would have autonomy over health care services and educators would have autonomy over curriculum, both of which would then be implemented through the bureaucratic structure (Clarke & Newman, 1997). This postwar settlement addressed complex social issues that could not be resolved by simple political or bureaucratic solutions. The role of the professional was a critical part of delivering social welfare services, as these experts provided the judgment needed to deliver ethical and appropriate services. The bureaucratic structure in turn provided the rules and procedures for implementing services in a fair and impartial manner. The combination of professionalism and bureaucratic administration helped to create a trusted system for delivering social services (Clarke & Newman, 1997).

This change in the function of the state that provided delivery of social welfare services, prevented future geopolitical rivalries, and implemented state economic regulations designed to prevent another depression is generally referred to as "embedded liberalism" (Harvey, 2005, p. 11). All such state forms of government had similar aims—that the state would intervene in industrial policy to spur economic growth, provide full employment, and provide a basic social welfare system. Embedded liberalism was the clear nexus of a social welfare state based in bipartisan support for a social ideology that established a clear bond between the state and the people. The state system of service delivery was based on professionalism and bureaucratic implementation and committed to public service (Clarke & Newman, 1997).

By the end of the 1960s, embedded liberalism was beginning to falter. On the economic front, the socioeconomic arrangement that had produced high growth rates since the end of World War II was no longer having such positive results (Harvey, 2005). Stagflation, or high unemployment rates coinciding with high inflation rates, created an economic emergency that led to a global recession lasting through most of the 1970s. There was a stagnating polarization of political-economic views during this time in the United States and other Western nations, and no economic solution was found that would create the conditions of capital accumulation needed to bring the economy out of the recession (Harvey, 2005).

It is important to note the economic and social impact of the three decades of welfare state policies on the global economy. During this time, there was a significant decrease in the income gap between whites and people of color. Increased costs of education and social services decreased corporate profits, a cause of concern for the corporate elite (Hursh & Henderson, 2011). There was an increase in the strength of organized labor, and a redistribution of wealth away from the wealthy and toward the working class. The impact of these changes were felt on a global scale (Harvey, 2005). As the economic elite were losing wealth to the working class, there was a simultaneous global shift to the political left, with power gains by the communist and socialist parties (Harvey, 2005). To the elite, this political shift threatened an even greater loss of wealth that, combined with the global shrinking of capital accumulation during the 1970s, put them in an unfamiliar position. Finding themselves in a vulnerable and uncomfortable situation, the economic elite felt they needed to act decisively to save themselves from losing even more of their wealth (Harvey, 2005).

The stagflation of the 1970s hurt all social sectors, but the global recession and lack of a solution to economic stagnation, combined with the growing financial threat to the wealthy class, set the stage for the dismantling of the postwar welfare state. In its place would be the introduction and implementation of a global neoliberal agenda, a project intended to restore class power to the wealthy, while antithetically appealing to the working class. The success of the project in recent decades has been nothing less than staggering. In the first two decades following the implementation of neoliberal policies in the United States, the share of the national income of the top one percent of income earners had almost doubled; the share of the top 0.1 percent had more than tripled. This hyper-concentration of wealth among the economic elite and away from the working class was not a US phenomenon but a global trend (Harvey, 2005).

The collapse of the postwar welfare state was not due solely to global economics and fear of a further redistribution of wealth. The last decade of the welfare state was also a time of changing family life. More mothers were engaged in paid employment, divorce and remarriage rates increased, and there was a rise in the number of single-parent households as well as gay, lesbian, and communal family arrangements (Clarke & Newman, 1997). Even with the increased social services available in the welfare state, rape, child abuse, and other forms of domestic violence were on the rise, and public social spending was increasingly seen as un-productive. There was also a growing mistrust of the supposed bureaucratic-professional neutrality of the welfare state. Instead of being seen as a professional and impartial system for imple-mentation of services, the bureaucratic structures of the social welfare state were increasingly seen as ineffective and impersonal. Professionals in the welfare state were increasingly viewed as being out of touch with reality and were blamed for growing social problems, rather than being seen as respected experts offering trusted judgments (Clarke & Newman, 1997).

In addition to these factors, there was one simple yet profound force that propelled neoliberalism to its current dominant world status: its commonsense aspect. This is a sense intuitive to the common person, which enables the theory to be interpreted as real regardless of whether its foundation is sound or flawed. Neoliberalism has been paired with a dominant, and to this day, remarkably persistent political plan (H. A. Giroux, 2014a), a commonsense narrative that has replaced the once-held global ideology of the social welfare state with the free-market ideology of neoliberalism. Narratives are rational story lines, and a well-told story can teach people to see the world differently. A narrative that has the ability to transform or replace one ideology with another may be said to have epistemic privilege (Somers & Block, 2005). Epistemically privileged ideas "come equipped with their own internal claims to veracity" (Somers & Block, 2005, p. 265). This does not mean they will automatically be accepted; the conversion narrative from one ideology to another is in fact a relatively rare occurrence, as people must decide for themselves whether a proposed idea makes sense to them. Somers & Block (2005) outline three requirements for a successful conversion: the narrative must first demonstrate why the existing ideology fails, then explain how intelligent people could have been misled, and, finally, offer a compelling alternative.

The turbulent economic climate of the 1970s provided rich fodder for the conversion narrative that helped supplant the apparently failing social welfare state with an unfettered free-market ideology. This narrative claimed that the public was "duped" by the ivory tower professionalism and inefficient bureaucracy of the social welfare state, and by the lack of social improvements resulting from thirty years of public investment (Somers & Block, 2005). With the narrative's underlying Malthusian perversity thesis as a theoretical foundation, shifting the blame for societal ills from poverty to the perversity of individuals, proponents of neoliberal theory successfully suggested that support for the populations that benefited from the welfare state was misguided. Arguing that the provisions of the welfare state in fact intensified poverty and other social problems, they proposed an alternative narrative of rugged individual self-reliance to replace one of individuals who were reliant on the state. To many, this commonsense narrative was quite compelling (Somers & Block, 2005). The argument was made, and won, that government policy was spending too much on supporting the poor, that state policy should instead emphasize employment and market fundamentalism. In terms of education policy, the conservative right claimed that the liberal education curriculum had been destroyed due to pressure from minority groups, and that this inadequate curriculum left students ill-prepared for the job market, which led to unemployment and poverty (Paraskeva, 2007). Given the claim that market fundamentalism is an empirical science, Somers and Block (2005) argue that the epistemic privilege and seeming invincibility of the conversion narrative for neoliberal ideology is nothing less than puzzling. Despite the contradictions of market fundamentalism in practice, neoliberal ideology has maintained its commonsense ethic and its preeminent location as a dominant philosophy.

The New Public Managerialism: Remaking the Form and Function of the State

In addition to converting ideological perceptions of the welfare state, the conversion of state organizational structures was also necessary for a fully successful transformation. In the globalized economy, the role of the state would also have to change, transformed from being a primary administrator of social services and public protections to serving as a more repressive force of control (Hill & Kumar, 2012). This process began as a quest for efficiency within the existing framework and moved on to marketization and the privatization of public resources and services. A new managerialism was born to govern state social services (Clarke & Newman, 1997). Emphasis was placed on setting target outcomes, defining metrics to measure those outcomes, and providing merit awards to those who achieved their goals. This competitive structure fostered a new form of public entrepreneurship that blurred the line between public and private. Managerial powers were limited by rules and procedures, and the organizational structures of the changing social welfare state had little to say about the social consequences of policy changes (Clarke & Newman, 1997). This new state form of managerialism was dependent on competitive entrepreneurialism and consumer freedom to make individual choices. These individual choices would be made without consideration of the greater collective social consequences.

A fundamental tenet of neoliberal ideology is the powerful notion of individual freedom. After all, who would not strive to be free? The state strongly favors an individual's freedom of choice, including the right to choose what they want to do and say and how they want to express themselves. The neoliberal state also favors strong individual property ownership rights (Harvey, 2005). An important aspect of the theory is the state's recognition of groups of people, including businesses and corporations, as individuals, which endows collective groups with the same rights of freedom as those held by individuals. The state supports free trade, free markets, and the "individual" rights of institutions to operate freely in such markets. Competition and free-market trade among individuals and companies, and between territorial entities such as cities, states, nations, and global regions, are viewed as a fundamental good (Harvey, 2005).

The neoliberal state supports entrepreneurial activity, innovation, and the creation of wealth. It is a primary responsibility of the state to support and protect individual freedoms, rights, and freedom of choice, as well as the "individual" rights of corporations, at all costs. The theory asserts that the state, operating in accordance with financialized business principles, should continually reorganize in ways that will produce efficiencies and competitive advantages. It promotes the unfettered mobility of capital between individuals, government sectors, countries, and global regions, which includes removing all barriers to the free movement of capital, goods, and services. Neoliberalism professes that competition, privatization, and deregulation will "eliminate bureaucratic red tape, increase efficiency and productivity, improve quality, and reduce costs" (Harvey, 2005, p. 65). The neoliberal state believes in private property rights as opposed to collective public property rights, and, thus, in the privatization of public goods to protect against individuals who might exploit common resources. It contends that sectors run by the state should be privatized and run by private enterprise (Harvey, 2005).

While individual freedom is accorded to all, each individual is also held accountable for their personal/private well-being, including being responsible for their own healthcare, education, and pensions. Individual successes are viewed as stories of entrepreneurial success. Individual failure is characterized as a personal rather than a public or structural failing. Individual failure, no matter the cause, is attributed to an individual's poor character, ability, or laziness. Neoliberal ideology professes that state sovereignty should be replaced by the sovereignty of free markets, and that increased productivity will "trickle down" to all of society; it holds that this process embodies the best way to eliminate poverty and provide for all. Some have used the adage that a "rising tide lifts all boats" (Harvey, 2005, p. 66), arguing that if the overall economy is doing well and productivity is high for most, then all will be lifted by the tide of prosperity. This theory fails to account for the individual who has no boat.

Neoliberal theorists hold that the fundamental principles of democracy and majority rule are contradictory to individual rights. Even if a majority votes in the best interests of the majority of individuals, that vote is seen as infringing on the rights and freedoms of an individual who is in the minority. The neoliberal instead believes it is far better for decisions to be made not by majority vote of the populace, but by executives, elites, and the judiciary; such decisions also serve to insulate key elite entities, such as banks, and both public and private institutions, from public pressure. In this scenario, it is up to the individuals in conflict with decisions made by the courts and executives to seek resolution through the courts (Harvey, 2005).

The individual choices and freedoms associated with the new managerialism, even if they do not represent true freedom for the vast majority, have transferred functions and responsibilities from the state to individuals. This redistribution of agency empowers the individual to provide for their own social welfare while subjecting them to the constraints and obligations of responsibility once provided by the bureaucratic-professional regime. While this dispersal of power in the form of individual freedom is empowering, it also is a form of control and imposed discipline (Clarke & Newman, 1997), as it transfers not only the power once held by the state but also the individual responsibility to the citizen-consumer. Managerialism is the governing ideology behind the dispersal of power to individuals. In transferring power from a system of governmental bureaucratic-professionalism to individuals, managerialism provides an efficient system for claiming corporate freedoms through the exercise of individual freedoms. By doing so, management prerogative reigns over the professional, resulting in a seemingly contradictory result: while individual responsibility and freedom may appear to be a retreat from state power, they in effect reflect an increase of state managerial power, one exercised in new and dispersed forms (Clarke & Newman, 1997). This dispersal of power to multiple individual stakeholders renders managerial decisions and power unstable. Insofar as individual freedoms are a structural element of neoliberal ideology, the instability caused by the dispersal of power is a structured instability, and insofar as the new managerialism constitutes an increase of state power that formulates the boundaries of stakeholder rights, it is the managerial state that defines a "hierarchy of legitimate interests" (Clarke & Newman, 1997, p. 32). In this structurally unstable scheme, with its strengthened power relations, understanding the contradiction between the theory and practice of freedom is of vital importance.

In light of this contradiction, one may well ask again who would not strive to be free. To answer that question, we must identify the type of freedom to which we are referring. Writing in 1944, Polanyi referred to both "good" and "bad" freedoms (Harvey, 2005, p. 36). Among the good, he listed freedom of speech and freedom of association. Among the bad were the freedom to exploit others and to profit from the misfortunes of others. All good and bad freedoms existed before the 1929 financial collapse and they still do today (Harvey, 2005), but the good freedoms have again been overwhelmed by the bad. Years of neoliberal freedom have "restored power to a narrowly defined capitalist class. They have also produced immense concentrations of corporate power" (Harvey, 2005, p. 38).

Describing the character of neoliberalism entails several challenges. There are many contradictions between its ideological foundation and the inconsistent ways it has been implemented (Saltman, 2012). One significant contradiction is the exemption of certain entities, such as the world's largest financial institutions, from competition. The fundamental neoliberal ethic of individual accountability mandates that individuals—including 'individual' financial institutions—be held accountable for their failings, yet many corporate entities have been exempted from such responsibility. As recently as the 2008 financial collapse, major US financial institutions were bailed out with taxpayer dollars because they were determined to be too large to fail (H. A. Giroux, 2014a). This practice of giving competitive favoritism to private capital cannot be reconciled with neoliberal theory. A similar contradiction is in tax policy regarding the added value obtained from the use of capital. While the state share of such revenue has remained constant since 1970, the private share has risen, due to corporate favoritism resulting from public-private partnerships (Harvey, 2012). Given such blatant preferential treatment of major financial institutions, it is clear who is in control—there is in fact no apparent effort to hide such overt favoritism. With subprime mortgage businesses, the exploitation of natural resources, and profiteering in valuable urban neighborhoods, there is no slowing of the financial pillaging despite the hundreds of financial crises that have occurred since 1973 (Harvey, 2012).

Before the 1970s, capital had assumed the cost of the structures and activities that supported social reproduction. Since about 1980, the goal "has been to dump these costs into the global commons of social reproduction and the environment, creating, as it were, a negative commons in which whole populations are now forced to dwell" (Harvey, 2012, p. 85). While the foundational basis of neoliberalism in theory is the "invisible hand" of the market, in reality it is the "visible hand" of politically and economically dominant corporations that has guided the contemporary global economy. This visible hand has been returning the economy to its pre-World War II status of unfettered accumulation of wealth. However, it is not so much the theory of neoliberalism as its fraudulent application in recent decades that has led to the current concentration of wealth. This improper relationship has ensured that the power elite faces no competition in the supposedly free market, an application of neoliberalism that stands in stark contrast to the theory itself (Harvey, 2012). This conflict between neoliberal theory and how it has been applied over the past four decades tells a story of greed, of bad freedoms run amok.

The application of neoliberalism in recent decades "should be understood as a tool of class warfare waged by the rich on the rest" (Saltman, 2012, p. 98). Implementation of the theoretical ideals of neoliberalism has been hijacked—or perhaps such ideals never existed but in the minds of economic purists. In their place has been a project that has significantly restored class power to the wealthy. As US investment guru Warren Buffett famously stated, "Sure there is a class war, and it is my class, the rich, who are making it and we are winning" (Harvey, 2012, p. 53). Decades of unfettered market orthodoxy have led to a severe erosion of economic security and, for many, to the loss of hope for a better future. Wealth inequality has increased. While those in the top earning categories have seen great increases in their income, during the first decades of neoliberal policies, the lowest 20 percent of US families in terms of income have seen no increase (Hill & Kumar, 2012). Even after the economic meltdown of 2008, economic recovery has been focused on restoring class power to the financial elite, not to the working class. In the first four years after the 2008 collapse, 91 percent of all new wealth in the United States was garnered by the top one percent of the wealthiest individuals. As a result, there is more wealth inequality today and a widely held understanding that the American economy no longer works for most (Stiglitz, 2015).

Neoliberalism is not healthy. Its fundamental goal is purportedly the well-being of all, but in recent decades household incomes in the United States have only grown due to the increase in two-worker households. In real dollars, men earn less than their fathers did (Hursh & Henderson, 2011). So, while proponents claim that all will be lifted by neoliberal policies, the real consequence of policy passing as neoliberalism has been the restoration of class power and the concentration of wealth among the financial elite. This conflict is dramatic—and makes it difficult to even use the term "neoliberalism" if you know its true meaning. The "nationalism required for the state to function effectively as a corporate and competitive entity in the world market gets in the way of market freedoms more generally" (Harvey, 2005, p. 79). The neoliberal monopoly of power contradicts the expectation of free-market competition. No matter the example, it is important to identify such inconsistencies and understand them for what they truly reflect—a misappropriated economic system being used to consolidate and protect the wealth of the elite class.

There have been attempts over the past forty years to claim that decision-making has been depoliticized, taken out of the political realm and put in the hands of managers who are empowered to oversee the efficient operation of services, free of political beliefs. Managers with centralized control have striven toward isomorphism, exhibiting a tendency to adopt a commonly accepted, standardized organizational form (Clarke & Newman, 1997). More specifically, there has been a decreasing tolerance among agencies delivering public services for formative differences that result in a narrowing of organizational structures. This tendency toward isomorphism has created a core business template with a focus on narrow outcomes associated with that template, as opposed to a broader public purpose (Clarke & Newman, 1997).

The focus on competition has also had detrimental effects, particularly in the public service sector, where there is competition to produce measurable social service outcomes with reduced resources. This has produced greater organizational efficiency, but individuals now bear the cost burden formally borne by the public, which has led to increased poverty and changed its social composition. The question arises of how business efficiency and a standardized isomorphic organizational structure impact or should impact the delivery of services related to social welfare. In addition, with free-market power being dispersed among multiple individuals, there has been a "dispersal of public services into a multiplicity of 'core businesses'" (Clarke & Newman, 1997, p. 155), whose fragmentation makes the agencies providing public services less effective and reveals significant concerns about public security. There is no longer a single state entity that claims to speak for the public interest, and this disintegration of the postwar welfare state into multiple fragmented agencies leaves many competing and singular interests that are competing for their own survival, none of which can claim to be seeking social cohesion, speaking for the public realm, or providing a broad degree of social security (Clarke & Newman, 1997).

These circumstances appear more severe when considering the condition of the state and its transformation over recent decades into an entity with rules, but where the enforcement of those rules is less than complete and evenly distributed, and where those rules have exceptions. A "state of exception" refers to a regime that has laws that have been suspended, a zone situated between law and life, like a civil war—in essence, a state at the intersection of the existence and application of law. A state of exception is a place where the law remains in force but its application has been suspended, a place where fact and law are indistinguishable from each other. A state of exception presents a paradox of existing simultaneously outside and within the state (Agamben, 2005). The period following World War I was one of great experimentation regarding the state of exception, and of testing state policies and government mechanisms that supported the state of exception. One lasting tradition of the period was partial eradication of the distinction between the executive, legislative, and judicial powers of state. With no separation of powers, one party can act unilaterally to suspend the application of laws, thus establishing the state of exception as a state paradigm (Agamben, 2005). Examples of states of exception include Hitler's Third Reich and the US internment of seventy thousand American citizens of Japanese descent during World War II. Each of these events was temporary, but each was an example of how

> modern totalitarianism can be defined as the establishment, by means of the state of exception, of a legal civil war that allows for the physical elimination not only of political adversaries

but of entire categories of citizens who for some reason cannot be integrated into the political system. Since then, the voluntary creation of a permanent state of emergency (though perhaps not declared in the technical sense) has become one of the essential practices of contemporary states, including so-called democratic ones.

(Agamben, 2005, p. 2)

The state of exception is closely related to the state of necessity. Agamben (2005, p. 24) cites the Latin proverb, "necessity has no law," which can be interpreted to mean that necessity does not recognize any law or that it creates its own. Either can be read as an interpretation of the state of exception, where laws exist but are not enforced. Necessity is a basic element of the validity of state of exception mandates, and it also legitimates austerity measures as a component of state government. Even when not imposed by state decree, state austerity measures—as in the form of reduced investment due to necessity—are to all intents and purposes a form of decree that impacts state policy decisions. In this case, "de facto proceedings, which are in themselves extra- or antijuridical, pass over into law, and juridical norms blur with mere fact—that is, a threshold where fact and law seem to become undecidable" (Agamben, 2005, p. 29). In such a case, the relation between the state of exception and the austerity politics of neoliberal ideology is clear.

The state of exception confuses several forces, such as executive and legislative powers, or austerity measures and law. Agamben (2005) claims it is critical to understand the separation between the force of law and the law itself. In one case, the law is in force yet not applied. Consider the inverse, where an assertion is not based in law yet it carries the force of law. In this case, the force of law "floats as an indeterminate element that can be claimed both by the state authority . . . and by a revolutionary organization" (Agamben, 2005, p. 38). It is in this sense of the state of exception that the force of law, without being a law, may become a tool of oppression in a space devoid of law, where no distinction is made between public and private, or legitimate and illegitimate authority. In the United States, the state of exception has been accompanied by a transformation from the post-World War II social welfare state to a seemingly permanent state of emergency—in other words, a state of necessity that has mandated cuts in social spending and caused a de facto manufactured change in social welfare policy. As such, "key concepts and practices—such as democracy, state, schooling, etc.—have been cleverly and gradually twisted and perverted, positively hijacked from the social sphere, and coined within an economic flavoured materiality" (Paraskeva, 2007, p. 137). This gradual perversion of the role of the state and the political impact of the state of exception cannot be separated from the dismantling of the post-World War II social welfare state. The shifting of blame from society to the individual is a unique consequence of the changed role of the state. Equal opportunity has been replaced by accountability—and by punishment for individuals who do not perform as expected. In education, this manifests as a "manic obsession with national testing" (Paraskeva, 2007, p. 154), a dangerous obsession with accountability over professionalism. Such accountability measures have been tied to state policy, disinvestment in public education, and a transfer of funding to private corporate entities (Saltman, 2012). As for the transformation of the state, such policies have seemingly inextricably linked the public with the private, creating public-private partnerships that have served the financial desires of private industry. In short, private enterprise has found a profitable new market in the public sector. But where there are winners there are also losers. The privatization of state functions has been accompanied by disinvestment in the public. With the increased private profits derived from public investment has come an increase in public debt and a further widening of the economic divide between the wealthy and the poor (Paraskeva, 2007).

The ideology of neoliberalism rests on the foundational claim that the well-being of all people is best served by liberating individual freedoms in a world of free markets and private property rights (Harvey, 2005). This market-based ethic requires interplay between the notions of individual freedom, a free-market economy, and private property. A fundamental tool of this relationship, and thus of neoliberalism, is the debtor-creditor relationship. In the past four decades, market individualism has expanded as an ethic to such an extent that individuals, corporations, and governmental organizations acting and being received as individuals have successfully striven to accumulate capital and property. The primary tool for this accumulation has been the financialization of the world economy through a massive accumulation of debt with private creditors. A critical factor to consider in the debt economy is the power differential in the debtor-creditor relationship (Lazzarato, 2012).

The neoliberal ethic situates all individuals in the position of the consumer, whose job is to serve society by accumulating not only physical merchandise but all elements of a social life, including entertainment, housing, health care, and education. This ethic is practiced in an environment of individual entrepreneurship, of "casino capitalism" if you will (H. A. Giroux, 2014a), where individuals take on the costs, risks, and debts associated with individual advancement. This consumptive and competitive society is based on the economic ethic of debt accumulation, where every debtor is in an unequal power relationship with their creditors. In this relationship, individuals are held accountable not to themselves but to the holders of capital. A primary product of this power structure, the indebted person, now occupies all public spaces in a debt-fueled economy (Lazzarato, 2012).

Entire countries as well as individuals are subject to this plan. The recent economic crisis in Europe is an example, where the economically weaker countries of the European Union such as Greece, Ireland, and Portugal find themselves replacing lost tax revenue by becoming indebted to private banks in countries like France and Germany (Lazzarato, 2012). These indebted countries now find themselves held hostage by the actions of rating agencies, which by lowering a governmental agency's bond rating can seemingly arbitrarily increase its interest payments. This predatory practice has in essence served as a form of public extortion, extracting money from economically weak debtor nations and delivering it to economically elite private entities, all in the name of avoiding a financial crisis (Lazzarato, 2012).

Current crises, whether individual, collective, or national, are indicative of the power differential between creditors and debtors. This imbalance of power has been used as an instrument of exploitation by helping creditors appropriate the wealth and labor of others. Such appropriation via the creation of debt is at the strategic heart of free-market politics, encompassing all individuals as accumulators of debt. Within this dynamic, the debtor-creditor relationship has become as much about morality as economics (Lazzarato, 2012). Debt brings debtors feelings of guilt, the sense that they are at fault, and the suspicion that others will believe they are lazy and caused their own self-imposed indebtedness. As the universal power relation of the unfettered free-market economy, debt projects guilt and shame on all. The morality-debt relationship is made all the more insidious when considering the impact financialization has had on social services such as housing, healthcare, and education (Lazzarato, 2012). Services once provided by the state are now commonly privatized and converted to debt. Real estate loans convert housing into debt, private insurance converts healthcare into debt, and college tuition loans convert higher education into debt. Payment for such services places the burden of the social on the individual. The universality of debt cuts across all social and political domains and is far too great to pay off given existing resources (Berardi, 2012; Lazzarato, 2012). This debt acts "as a condition for the final predatory abstraction: life turned into time for repaying a metaphysical debt. Life, intelligence, joy, breathing—humanity is going to be sacrificed in order to pay the metaphysical debt" (Berardi, 2012, p. 25). Lazzarato (2012) argues further that even trying to pay one's debt is an admission of guilt, and as such the debt should not be repaid. He claims that the accumulated debt with its associated guilt "is not an economic problem but an apparatus of power designed not only to impoverish us, but to bring about catastrophe" (Lazzarato, 2012, p. 164). In short, we have reached an untenable managerial-neoliberal state of affairs, in which the societal elements of living have been transformed into an unsustainable fiscal debt, a yoke which weighs on the social elements of living a safe and productive life.

To consider alternatives, to imagine reversing the current power structures of the financialized world where all human existence and interaction are reduced to transaction (Harvey, 2005), we must understand our current condition. The accelerated, hyper-complex, and chaotic flows of information exchange transformed by neoliberal practices have come to define the environment and conditions of human existence. The extraction and accumulation of capital from capital, as opposed to capital from the production of goods, has become intimately related to the virtualization of human intellect (Berardi, 2012). Financialization has become so ingrained in the fabric of human existence that the distinction between money and life has been blurred. Human interaction and social life have been reduced to a financial algorithm, yet no such algorithm is suited to organize and maintain a multilayered, dynamic, and complex existence. Language and learning have become technological phenomena. Human relations are governed by the financial arrangement of debt, yet debt "is an act of language, a promise" (Berardi, 2012, p. 31). These contradictions between the foundational elements of social human life and financial capitalization must be fully understood in context in order to make sense of neoliberalism as the dominant ideology of human existence. To gain this understanding, one must dissociate the elements and discern their relationships, as well as their impact on each other and on the human condition. In so doing, one may expose their fundamental connections and how they serve as the foundational basis of neoliberal ideology. These contradictions between human relations and finance are ingrained in our current existence. Attempts have been made to separate financial influence from human existence, but peaceful protest, while effective in democratic structures, has proven ineffective in the current situation, where "techno-financial automations have taken the place of political decisions" (Berardi, 2012, p. 53). Social movements have been successful in the past, but social solidarity is not a part of the daily practice of today's citizenry. There are many reasons for this. The hyper-acceleration of social and brain power production in the knowledge economy has pushed the professional and economic endeavors of work into daily social and personal spaces. The changing role of the worker and the working mother has impacted the upbringing of our children, including the ways they learn and communicate (Berardi, 2012).

In this process, human ability to fully understand and interpret the surrounding world has been diminished (Berardi, 2012). This downgrading of human faculties has caused a verifiable decline in the efficiency of economic production, which has called attention to a dramatic increase in reports of mental illness (Davies, 2011). In short, performance measures show that human well-being is suffering in the current capitalist world environment. The decrease in economic productivity associated with mental health issues demonstrates that the current situation is impacting both human productivity and happiness, and that there is indeed a correlation between the two. Cognitive behavioral therapy has proven effective in addressing workplace inefficiency. It also has been shown that going to work can have a positive effect on human happiness, which indicates that human interaction such as that in the workplace can be a therapeutic measure. There is clear evidence of the positive correlation between the political economy and happiness (Davies, 2011).

All of these factors have influenced the current situation of human existence within a market-based reality. Fueled by the abstraction of money, with exchange value no longer connected to physical usefulness, we have graduated to a world where humanity is reduced to automation over human activity, technology over intellect and imagination. Such changes have impacted intellectual and creative elements of human social existence, such as linguistics and poetry. While such artistic language as poetry cannot be reconciled in a system of financial exchange, what it can do is "escape from the matrix and reinvent a social sphere of singular vibrations intermingling and projecting a new space for sharing, producing, and living" (Berardi, 2012, p. 147). Only in such a space can an act of language create a new life form, and, in so doing, reactivate the intellect, challenging and transforming the concrete limits of financial capitalism. In this space, intellectual and linguistic activity has the capacity to confront limit situations defined by financial capital (Berardi, 2012, p. 157). This space also allows the intellectual, the poet, and the linguistic actor to claim their voice or, as Freire (2000, p. 88) wrote, to "speak their word" and to thereby confront the oppressor with an act capable of transforming a limit previously defined as a barrier into one defined as a place where a multitude of possibilities begin. This concept will come into play in later chapters, as we consider the connection between education and vocation, notably, how language, communication, and creativity are critically important in an education that prepares a student for both life and vocation in a technological world.

We have now considered the tenets of neoliberalism and its global implementation over the past four decades. We understand the seemingly logical conversion narrative that helped transform the formerly dominant social welfare state into the current globally dominant market ideology. We have examined the commonsense hegemony that has helped make neoliberal ideology so dominant, and the new form of managerialism that has tended toward isomorphic uniformity. With this understanding, we will now move on to examine how market ideology has impacted colleges and universities, and, perhaps most importantly, how the new managerialism of the neoliberal age has come to dominate higher education. It is reasonable to consider such an application of neoliberalism apart from its definition and consider whether such an application or its theoretical counterpart may have any progressive impact on society or on the social construct of education policy. We have so far seen that neoliberalism has run amok and been claimed by a political project to reestablish the dominance of the financial elite. As we investigate the status of higher education, we should now keep our minds open to both its theory and application.

2 The New Political Economy of Higher Education

In this chapter, I examine the historical role of US colleges and universities, including the longstanding tradition of their being operated using business principles. I investigate the historical partnership between faculty and college presidents that gave birth to the notions of shared governance and the faculty-administrator. I will trace the impact neoliberal ideology has had on these institutions, which I argue has led to the decline of the faculty-administrator and thus of shared governance, and also to the prominence of the professional administrator. My analysis will examine the past and present state of university governance structures, taking into account faculty involvement in academic and institutional decisions as well as the impact the new managerialism in higher education has had on such governance structures. Finally, I investigate the sometimes-contradictory circumstances of corporate-university partnerships and the historical social and democratic purposes of higher education.

In the United States, public higher education operates under different administrative structures than public elementary and secondary schools. One main difference is in the funding structure, as—in contrast with fully funded elementary and secondary education—the cost of higher education is only partially supported by tax revenues, in this case by state appropriations (Center for the Study of Education Policy, 2015). The remaining funding comes from a variety of sources—student tuition and fees, grant money, and other fundraising derivations. Due to this dynamic, it is commonly accepted that higher education institutions—whether public or private—are run like businesses. Mimicking business jargon, the college or university president is often referred to as the chief executive officer (CEO), one of whose primary functions is widely understood to be raising money (Ginsberg, 2011). The corporate structure and free-market ethos that have come to dominate higher education in recent decades have become commonplace modes of institutional governance. This transformation has been accomplished by a well-orchestrated plan that includes

> the squelching of academic freedom, the rise of an ever increasing contingent of part-time faculty, the rise of a bloated managerial class, and the view that students are basically consumers and faculty providers of a saleable commodity such as a credential or a set of workplace skills. More striking still is the slow death of the university as a center of critique, vital source of civic education, and crucial public good.
>
> (H. A. Giroux, 2014a, p. 16)

As is the case throughout the dominant Western culture, the sense of moral responsibility and concern for the welfare of others have been severely diminished. The hegemony of individualism, economic Darwinism, and anti-public rhetoric has come to dominate the discourse of higher education, as it has the larger society.

Operating as a business signifies a commodification of certain aspects of college and university existence. Students may be equated with a positive monetary value represented by the intake of tuition dollars, while faculty, librarians, deans, and other employees may be equated with a negative monetary value represented by expenditures—all of which can be summarized in a financial spreadsheet (Ginsberg, 2011). The notion that these aspects of educational enterprise can be associated with financial transactions may be alarming to those who view their role in the educational environment to be anything but transactional. Nevertheless, the commodification of faculty, students, services, and every other aspect of college life is in fact in accordance with the dominant neoliberal ideology prevalent in society since the 1970s (Harvey, 2005). Those who govern the modern-day university—the trustees, the president, and many other administrators—are often selected for their business acumen and entrepreneurial ingenuity, much as those who govern in industry are selected. Trustees in particular represent a powerful force that connects industry and the university, and provide a mediating influence between the public and private sectors (Slaughter & Rhoades, 2004).

The Origins and Development of Shared Governance

The tradition of higher education institutions raising money and operating like corporations is in fact a longstanding condition. Writing over one hundred years ago, Veblen (1918) likened the new breed of college president to being the CEO of a major corporation, referring to their entrepreneurial business ethos, and calling them "captains of erudition." Veblen wrote at a time when enrollment in higher education was increasing on a dramatic scale. Hungry for tuition dollars, this increase was welcomed by these captains of erudition, but expanding their institutions came at a cost, including the need for more faculty and administrators (Ginsberg, 2011). The rapid rise in the number of students, faculty, administrators, and staff members fundamentally changed the character of the institution, and led to the need for the administration to cooperate with the faculty in expanding programs and curriculum. Aggressive administrators, eager to expand, began to use faculty as leaders and administrators throughout this process of expansion (Ginsberg, 2011). An academic department was considered the administrative unit of a given discipline. Within the department, faculty members wielded great power. To effect the changes they wanted, the captains of erudition agreed to relinquish some degree of power to faculty; this was the beginning of a partnership and the inception of what many now refer to as shared governance (Ginsberg, 2011).

During this time, higher education was increasingly seen as a necessity for those seeking a professional life. This perception helped fuel the increase in student enrollments and the resulting expansion of higher education. In the early twentieth century, as the captains of erudition were expanding their institutions to meet the growing interest in and demand for higher education, there was active debate about academic freedom for faculty (Ginsberg, 2011). The American Association of University Professors (AAUP) was established in 1915, with prominent scholar John Dewey as its first president. That same year, the AAUP proposed creating a tenure system that would give faculty a degree of academic freedom and job security, and allow them to speak freely and critically without fear of losing their jobs. Academic freedom, which had been debated since before the turn of the century, was a primary focus for the AAUP and its predecessor organizations. Colleges, universities, and their presidents opposed the tenure proposal; the presidents in fact created their own organization in response to the AAUP. Members of the American Association of Colleges (AAC) were unified in their opposition to the tenure proposal (Ginsberg, 2011). Then, in 1922, the AAC took a sharp change of course and accepted almost the entire AAUP tenure proposal. What may have been seen as a startling change of heart on the part of the presidents actually had more practical origins. Being captains of erudition, the presidents understood that they needed to attract, tolerate, and retain highly qualified faculty if they were to continue to expand their institutions to meet the future student demand. Without the promise of job security that came with tenure, faculty would be likely to leave a job and go with the highest bidder or best working conditions (Ginsberg, 2011). Moreover, the rapid growth of colleges and universities between 1915 and 1922 caused dramatic changes in the nature of these institutions. To cope and thrive in this changing environment, a different type of management was needed.

During this time, an increasing number of academics had become college presidents, and they were more inclined to understand and support tenure. Faced with larger faculties and their increased power in matters of institutional governance, college presidents recognized that a stable and happy faculty translated into stable colleagues and support structures (Ginsberg, 2011). So, while the AAC's 1922 decision may have seemed a dramatic shift, it was in reality a practical tradeoff to support the advancement and expansion of higher education. In the coming years, ever more pressure was put on higher education institutions to offer tenure to their faculty. In the 1940s and 1950s, college enrollments in the United States more than tripled, causing yet another hiring crisis and prompting most institutions to offer tenure. Within the next two decades, 80 percent of full-time faculty held tenured or tenure-track positions (Ginsberg, 2011).

The unprecedented changes in faculty governance that took place in the mid-twentieth century, including increased faculty influence over institutional decisions, also brought changes in the institutional mission. Changes in higher education had been further encouraged by two tumultuous world wars and the growing belief that higher learning needed to be accessible to more than just the privileged classes. There was recognition in at least some sectors that responsibility for making higher learning accessible to all did not rest solely with the university. According to Ortega (1944, p. 52), "the process of making the university accessible to the working man is only in small part the concern of the university; it is almost wholly the business of the state." The recognition that higher education has a civic purpose makes it necessary to consider both who is to be given access to higher learning and what type of education should be made available. The implicit understanding was that higher education was needed to train professionals to work in society—including

> judges, doctors, engineers—and therefore [that] the university is prepared to furnish professional training. But society needs

before this, and more than this, to be assured that the capacity is developed for another kind of profession, the profession of governing.

(Ortega, 1944, p. 58)

The word "governing" in this case does not necessarily signify a person who holds elected office or is some other way engaged in public governance, but one who is engaged in and influences their own community. It signifies the power in an educated professional's ability to impact the civic life of their community. Ortega's (1944) insistence that such educational opportunity be afforded not only to the elite but also to the working class foreshadows the discussion in the following two chapters of the new political economy of a community college education and its ability to support students' right to the city (Lefebvre, 1996).

Whether in the mid-twentieth century or the early twenty-first, it is critical to discern what type of education is needed to connect the educated person to their community's civic and cultural life. To foster this type of higher learning, institutions must engage in "the teaching of the culture, the system of vital ideas, which the age has attained. This is the basic function of the university. This is what the university must be, above all else" (Ortega, 1944, p. 59). An education with a narrow focus does not adequately prepare a person to act as a leader in society. The natural scientist, for example, must be conversant in the arts, and the healthcare professional must be conversant in the social sciences. To be a leader within their profession or in their cultural and social communities, a person needs a general education. Furthermore, the student must be the primary focus of a professional education. The institutional organization, "the construction of the university, must be based upon the student, and not upon the professor or upon knowledge" (Ortega, 1944, p. 70). This is the only way education can prepare a student to help shape and live fully in the conditions of their existence. In order to achieve such a student focus, decisions regarding curricula and pedagogy must fully engage faculty voice. It is one thing for education to be available to all, but the higher education institution must have a governance structure that includes faculty decision-makers and aims to create a university that is "open to the whole reality of its time . . . in the midst of real life, and saturated with it" (Ortega, 1944, p. 97).

Ortega's (1944) work may be viewed as a higher education application of work done by Dewey (2004) a generation earlier, and by

Freire (2000) and Lefebvre (1996) a generation later, as I discuss in later chapters. In 1916, Dewey (2004) made the essential connection between education and the social environment of democratic society. He stated that "a community or social group sustains itself through continuous self-renewal," namely, through an educational process in which "a society transforms uninitiated and seemingly alien beings into robust trustees of its own resources and ideals" (2004, p. 10). That a primary benefit of education is to support societal ideals was a new idea at the time, but it eventually gained a prominent place in the American education system. Dewey recognized that education could not rely solely on the detached dissemination of information to students and that the student must be an engaged participant in their own education. The environment in which learning takes place includes conditions and factors that both promote and create barriers to the learning process. This complex environment, which includes social elements and human relationships, connects educational processes to social and democratic ideals and structures. It recognizes that what an individual does and can do is impacted by their social and political interactions with others (Dewey, 2004). When new ideas are investigated and new knowledge is created, it should not be assumed that earlier learners were less able but that the social circumstances of the time did not guide them in what may now seem an obvious direction, and that earlier environmental factors may have pointed them in other directions considered fruitful at the time. This connection between student learning and the social environment may also be viewed in consort with issues of institutional shared governance. The faculty member who creates such a socially connected learning environment for their student must also be connected to democratic governance processes within the institution in which that learning takes place.

An individual learns by acquiring not just rote knowledge but applicable meaning, while involved in a social interaction that includes sharing a common experience with others. The social environment required for meaningful learning to take place "forms the mental and emotional disposition of behavior in individuals by engaging them in activities that arouse and strengthen certain impulses" (Dewey, 2004, p. 16). The socially prompted impulses that engage and guide individuals have a significant impact on what experiences may be stimulated in and shared by the learner; thus, the social environment of the educational process is both real and powerful. Based on this connection between learning and the social environment, Dewey (2004) concluded that the type of education an individual receives can be shaped through the influence of the social learning environment.

One hundred years later, it is apparent that US education policy has strayed from this understanding. Nevertheless, Dewey's principle is a foundational element of this study, as it connects the educational environment to the social and political environment. It mandates that social change be connected to educational processes, and that these processes, rather than being coercive, be intrinsically related to the identity and predispositions of the individual learner. Perhaps most importantly, it requires that schooling include a social environment with "more opportunity for conjoint activities in which those instructed take part, so that they may acquire a social sense of their own powers" (Dewey, 2004, p. 39). Viewing the learner as one element of a rich social environment demands consideration of the elements of society acted upon by the learner as they discover and confront their growing power to impact their environment. This consideration will enable us to understand the vital and interconnected relationship between the learner's learning process, support of democratic processes, and self-determination. If an educational institution hopes to create this kind of connected experience for its students, it must examine its governance processes to determine if the ideal of supporting democratic processes is fully embraced by the institution.

Educational institutions are microcosms of society. They connect learning not only to the individual but to each student's social efficacy, in part as this relates to self-determination. These institutions expose their students to democratic ideals and have the potential to foster democratic processes within their own institutional operations. This prompts a revisiting of the processes of institutional governance. One mystery of public higher education in the United States today is the overt absence of Dewey's democratic framework, or even his mitigated influence in the daily life of higher education. While the aim of this project is not to examine that mystery, I am compelled to point out the contradictions between current circumstances and some of the historical roots of US higher education, notably its expressed purpose of providing an education that would support post-World War II democratic society, as espoused by President Truman's Commission on Higher Education more than seventy years ago. The Truman Commission's vision has all but disappeared in recent decades (Schrum, 2007); perhaps, it represented only a fleeting ideal that has been overtaken by the economic greed of recent decades. With the annihilation of the progressive ideals and values endorsed by Dewey, Truman, and others at the institutional level (whether state or university), circumstances today fail to broadly reflect ideals that do not diverge from a democratic way of thinking and living. Any such democracy is democratic in name only. Wolf (2007) argues that this same mystery was perpetrated by Stalinism and Nazism, as both Stalin and Hitler used the very instruments of democracy to kill democracy, including the instrument of education.

The model of institutional governance born in Ortega's and Dewey's time and promoted by the captains of erudition in the early to mid-twentieth century lasted into the 1970s. In this model, faculty had a great deal to say about the direction of the institution and about new knowledge created, and had a vision for society (Ginsberg, 2011). Faculty often would "moonlight" as temporary administrators, and when their tour was over they would return to their faculty position and continue their teaching and research career. This was a common arrangement, and many faculty administrators served as department chairs, deans, provosts, and even occasionally as college presidents. This dynamic was beneficial to faculty, upper administration, and the institution itself. Perhaps most importantly, it ensured the integrity of academic programs by keeping them under the control of the curriculum experts (Ginsberg, 2011).

The Death of Shared Governance

Neoliberalism proposes that human well-being is best served through implementation of political and economic practices that promote individual responsibility, entrepreneurial freedom, private property rights, and open and free markets. The theory, which proposes that these free markets should serve both economic and socials purposes, was first broadly put into practice in the late 1970s and early 1980s, and was championed by world leaders Deng Xiaoping, Margaret Thatcher, Ronald Reagan, and US Federal Reserve chair Paul Volcker. Neoliberal ideology had been around for many years, but its wide-scale political practice was largely a new phenomenon (Harvey, 2005).

Entrepreneurial spirit has been exercised in higher education for at least a century, with college presidents operating their institutions in accordance with corporate business principles (Veblen, 1918). These principles are still applied today, but significant differences separate business principles from neoliberal principles as defined in

Chapter 1. Entrepreneurial freedom is alive and well at institutions employing the principles of shared governance, but it is a collective rather than individual freedom, with academic decisions subject to the checks and balances of shared authority that aims to preserve academic, disciplinary, and institutional integrity. Captains of erudition may guide such institutions that are bent on expansion and entrepreneurial pursuits, but only if those pursuits are consistent with sound academic foundations as determined by disciplinary experts. Analogously, faculty may guide an institution in a particular programmatic direction, but only as far as the direction and programs are consistent with sound business principles as determined by college administration. This collective decision-making process is not as fast and efficient as one individual making all decisions, but it is effective if an institution is concerned with making decisions that are sound from both a business and an academic perspective. Given these factors, shared governance—as signified by faculty content experts having significant power in setting institutional priorities and direction—is incompatible with neoliberal ideology's expression of "individual entrepreneurial freedoms."

Institutions employing the unfettered market mechanisms of current-day neoliberal practice to govern faculty work provide a striking contradiction to the social democratic processes of shared governance. The individualism of the market ethos contradicts a shared concern for society, including the foundational principles and purposes of a democratic education. Faculty engagement in governance mandates addressing an institutional purpose that is focused on the collective benefit of student learning, whereas the free-market ethos of neoliberalism prescribes that each element of the institution, including faculty members, strives for individual success, thus negating the foundational purpose of shared governance for the collective good of students.

Education is by nature a process for the collective good of students and the benefit of all society—not just one element of society. As such, the essential concept of neoliberal ideology that the well-being of all is best achieved by focusing on the individual is a bankrupt notion. Moreover, it is foundationally inconsistent with the concept of shared governance in an educational institution. This inconsistency pits the hegemonic power as applied in the current neoliberal state directly against the democratic power of shared governance. It is crucial to point out the differences between these uses of the word "power": hegemonic power connotes dominance, the ability to control in ways often hidden from view or understanding, while democratic power represents the capacity to influence in a transparent public forum. In an educational setting, the democratic power to influence has the ability to thwart the hegemonic dominance of neoliberalism.

Higher education has not been immune to the neoliberal practices that have since the 1970s gradually replaced concern for social responsibility with a focus on individual freedom and responsibility. The fundamental changes this has brought include a dramatic shift away from faculty and administration sharing the authority to govern the growth and direction of the institution; thus, the tradition of shared governance has been in serious decline over the past few decades (Ginsberg, 2011). Largely gone are the days when faculty would take an administrative position for a period of time and then return to their role as teacher and researcher. In fact, since the 1970s, higher education has experienced massive growth in the number of professional administrators. These are largely full-time managers, many with management degrees, who generally are not culled from faculty ranks; those who were former faculty members rarely plan to return to their former role (Ginsberg, 2011). This change has signified a compelling transfer of institutional power and decision-making away from professional educators and toward professional managers.

This transfer in recent decades has shifted power away from faculty and toward college presidents and their administrations (Bowen & Tobin, 2015), which signifies both a change in faculty status and a loss of sovereignty. Faculty do serve on governance committees, but committee work is often relegated to making recommendations to professional managers. Rather than faculty being autonomous professionals, the faculty/administration dynamic has grown closer to an employee/supervisor relationship. These changes have also brought a collective loss of sovereignty among unions and faculty senates (Aronowitz, 2000). The overall transformation has had a dramatic effect on higher education, specifically on the institutional structure and dynamics that influence institutional decisions. The marginalization of the faculty role and the enhanced role of the professional administrator have changed the face of higher education. This new management structure is not well suited to govern in this context, as it does not understand or appreciate the character and purpose of higher education (Ginsberg, 2011).

Along with this dramatic shift in institutional power, the number of administrators has increased at a much greater rate than that of faculty. There have also been critical changes in the ranks of professional support staff members whose function is to assist administrators in managing the institution (Ginsberg, 2011). From 1975 to 2005, full-time faculty at US colleges and universities increased by 51 percent, which is comparable to the increase in student enrollments, while the number of college and university administrators increased by 85 percent. Perhaps more telling, however, is the fact that professional support staff increased by 240 percent. This dynamic has greatly reduced the faculty role in institutional governance and created a disconnection between faculty and management. College administrations relied on faculty for most of the twentieth century, but they are now significantly more autonomous. They have wrested control of academic decisions away from the faculty and marginalized their influence. What had been a successful system of checks and balances through shared governance is largely gone, replaced by a system of non-academic professional managers charged with guiding all aspects of the institution, including academic decisions and direction.

Higher education today is dominated by professional administrators and their staff, who are generally neither curricular experts nor trained in pedagogical principles in the academic disciplines. After a time, even those who were faculty become isolated from and lose touch with the academic life, as they are almost forced by the system itself to give up their academic pursuits and become engulfed in the world of administration, often focused on making decisions based on financial resources and the need to find more. They also often find that engaging in these non-educational activities is necessary in order to climb to the next rung on the administrative ladder (Aronowitz, 2000). As career administrators become more detached from academic life, they may see themselves as part of a different educational social strata, which makes the transition from educator to supervisor complete. At universities across the country, this "permanent administrative bureaucracy in education was the crucial internal precondition for the gulf that now separates faculty and students from educational leaders, leading to the development of the corporate university" (Aronowitz, 2000, p. 164). In some contexts, this transformation has been complete, and many colleges and universities are now proud and unapologetic practitioners of corporate values. With these values has come a corporate management ethos that has reduced support for programs that are not directly business oriented and for research that is not considered profitable for the institution. Forms of shared governance are shunned in favor of business management principles (H. A. Giroux, 2014a).

Any attempt to remedy this current condition without addressing the issue of faculty governance and reengaging faculty in the academic decision-making process will be futile.

To a great extent, the public does not view colleges and universities as businesses, seeing them instead as entities of the public good. While this view belies many institutional realities, it correctly points to differences between the operation of a college or university and a corporate entity (Ginsberg, 2011). While the modern higher education institution employs many business principles, corporate decisions are largely dictated by profit, which is presumed to be less true in public ventures such as education. While corporate managers base their decisions on how they contribute to the company's fiscal security and growth, and are rewarded on such outcomes, with few opportunities for financial reward, higher education managers may be less likely to make decisions based on the interests of the institution than on their own interests and opportunity for advancement (Ginsberg, 2011). This may bring into question decisions about determining institutional direction, decisions which were formerly shared with faculty. Higher education management differs significantly from corporate management in this regard, as it exhibits work and decision-making strategies that are sometimes detached from the most important and foundationally relevant product of the institution: teaching, learning, and research. Ginsberg points to "make-work" activities—time-consuming demands such as attending meetings or conferences, meetings to plan meetings, as well as the ubiquitous strategic-planning process.

Government agencies and institution trustees, who often come from the business world, are accustomed to working from a strategic business plan. Strategic planning in higher education is less akin to a business plan than it is to an assertion of leadership and a claim to control institutional priorities and resources. A "real" business or strategic plan would likely include a list of concrete objectives, a timeline, an articulation of how the objectives might be achieved, assigned responsibilities for each part of the plan, and a budget (Ginsberg, 2011). In contrast, most higher education strategic plans are indistinguishable from one another, have vague goals, no budget, and are more a vision statement than a concrete plan. Although the concept of creating a strategic plan appears to fit the business model, in higher education practice it "is not a blueprint for the future. It is, instead a management tool for the present. The ubiquity of planning at America's colleges and universities is another reflection and reinforcement of the ongoing growth of administrative power" (Ginsberg, 2011, p. 52). We see in these examples that, while there are similarities between corporate and higher education management, there are also significant differences. These differences are both qualitative, in underlying motivations, and quantitative, in specific aspects of strategy and planning. While applying business principles to higher education may be sold in terms of institutional effectiveness, it can also end up co-opting institutional decision-making.

One area where higher education has clearly mimicked the corporate sector is in the use of part-time labor. Part-time adjunct instructors now teach the majority of classes at US colleges and universities. With institutions relying so heavily on this part-time labor force, some believe that these positions should no longer be considered as contingent labor, but that they have become a normalized reality (Aronowitz, 2000). With significantly lower salaries, no commitment to long-term employment, low overhead costs for typical faculty-/job-related expenses such as office space and health and retirement benefits, institutions are realizing a tremendous cost savings. On the other hand, another area where higher education veers from business principles is in what it does with these cost savings. Instead of lowering tuition costs or being invested in academic programs that support institutional goals, the cost savings have helped to pay for the dramatic increase in administration and support staff, including both more positions and higher salaries (Ginsberg, 2011).

An extreme example of the use of adjunct faculty, and of the changing role of faculty in both governance and instruction, is currently playing out at Southern New Hampshire University (SNHU). SNHU's College of Online and Continuing Education is piloting a program to serve its 37,000 online students. For this large population, SNHU employs 2,700 remote adjunct faculty members; it also plans to hire a mere forty-five full-time faculty. This will result in an astounding ratio of 600:1 adjunct to full-time faculty (Bowen & Tobin, 2015). These full-time faculty positions will not conform to traditional standards; like their adjunct counterparts, they will work remotely, not on campus. They will not be expected to publish, but will be expected to provide frequent feedback to their online students. There will be no formal long-term commitment to full-time faculty, as each will serve a one-year, non-tenure-track appointment, with no promise of the academic freedom expected with other full-time faculty positions. It is also not known whether full-time faculty will have any role in institutional governance.

Even more potentially damaging to the faculty role than a skewed faculty ratio or the lack of formal job security, SNHU has become widely known for being accredited to award degrees through competency based education (CBE). CBE students are assessed and then awarded credit based on what they can show they know, with little consideration of where that knowledge was gained or how long it took them to learn it (Klein-Collins, 2013). There also are no courses and no grades. This modality dramatically changes the nature of the faculty position, replacing the traditional faculty role with "coaches" who help students progress through the project-based online activity (Clerkin & Simon, 2014). Projects are designed in close cooperation with employers, enabling students to exhibit the skills and attributes desired in the workplace. SNHU also offers other online resources to help students successfully demonstrate their competencies (Clerkin & Simon, 2014). This is an extreme example of faculty losing control of the curriculum. In fact, it can be argued that a curriculum determined by faculty has been replaced by one designed to meet industry needs by focusing on students' workforce readiness. Rather than being evaluated by faculty, students will be coached through online evaluations that determine their college credits. SNHU is not only testing the boundaries of a dramatically increased use of adjunct faculty and the loss of faculty control of the curriculum, it is also fundamentally challenging the role of and the need for higher education faculty. As the SNHU project continues and other institutions explore the possibilities of CBE, it will be important to fully examine the impact not only on faculty but on student learning and on the liberal and democratic purposes of education.

Numerous other "innovative" higher education models seem to surface weekly. In a recent news story, a dean at the Massachusetts Institute of Technology (MIT) was reported to be taking a leave of absence in order to create a new university with no classrooms or lectures. Like SNHU, this new university would have a project-based learning model, with the foundational notion of putting all materials related to knowledge acquisition online (Young, 2016). This new university would follow the increasingly popular model of using non-tenure-track faculty. The entrepreneurial MIT dean believes she will be able to attract high-quality scholars to teach at the new university from among the glut of talented doctoral students and postdocs who are currently unable to secure full-time employment in academia due to the dearth of open positions (Young, 2016). These are just two of the numerous examples of higher education institutions that are transforming the role of faculty, and, thereby, the potential for faculty to be engaged in academic governance. The increasing use of part-time faculty has also had a significant impact on full-time faculty. Where faculty administrators had for decades been active leaders in decision-making, wielded great power in institutional direction, and served in an administrative layer that shielded upper administration from the trustees, the shift in institutional power, organization, and governance over the last four decades has taken away much of this shared governance and responsibility. With the loss of status and need for faculty administrators that has accompanied the increase of professional managers in higher education, along with the dramatic increase of part-time instructors, all faculty roles have changed. With the decreased role for full-time faculty and increased use of part-time faculty, institutions are now less likely to offer the academic freedom provided by granting tenure (Ginsberg, 2011). The increasing burden put on part-time instructors and the dramatic increase in professional administrators and staff have put full-time faculty in a tenuous position. The increasing number of part-time and non-tenured faculty, many of whom have little job security and fear loss of employment, "occupy the status of indentured servants who are overworked, lack benefits, receive little or no administrative support, and are paid salaries that qualify them for food stamps" (H. A. Giroux, 2014a, p. 20). Moreover, as a matter of course, they have very little power or voice in academic governance. The increasing number of full-time faculty who do not have tenure are experiencing a parallel loss of voice and lack of ability to critique academic decisions and governance processes. They find themselves separated from academic decision-making by a thickening layer of professional administrators, managers, and staff. Each of these situations reflects the conflicts that arise in what has become the dominant new political economy of higher education. This new economy, which has developed over the past four decades, has dramatically altered the long-term relationship between administration and faculty, and transferred academic decision-making power from faculty content experts to professional managers.

Another area where the faulty application of business principles is impacting education is in evaluating the performance of students, faculty, institutions, and systems of institutions. In the business world, individuals and divisions within businesses tend to be evaluated using economic measures related to income, cost, and profitability (Ginsberg, 2011). In public elementary and secondary schools, students, schools, districts, and, increasingly, teachers tend to be evaluated using the results of standardized tests. These assessment results are used to label, reorganize, close, and privatize public schools (Lipman, 2011). In higher education, performance assessment is far less structured and developed, although there is a growing movement toward outcomes assessment. Outcomes in this case are more than just the goals or objectives of a course or program; they are intended to measure a particular activity. Historically, assessing student performance was the prerogative of the course instructor, but, in recent years, college administrations have aligned themselves with accrediting agencies. This has given them a degree of leverage over faculty and enabled them to push for broader assessment measures using a broader group of assessors; no longer would an individual faculty member assess their own students (Ginsberg, 2011). Faculty face increasing pressure to develop measurable outcomes and create the assessment tools needed to measure whether students satisfy those outcomes. While standardized testing as found in elementary and secondary school is not yet required, some faculty may be concerned that outcomes assessment efforts may move further away from their own authentic assessment of student learning and toward a form of standardized testing, representing a form of control and a further loss of their authority to professional administrators. There is also concern that outcomes assessment is being used to further stratify higher education. Accrediting agencies have historically been able to "bully" lower-tier colleges and universities and community colleges, while the elite private institutions are able to ignore such initiatives, knowing that the accrediting agencies need them to maintain their own credibility (Ginsberg, 2011).

The university as a business has been contemplated since Veblen's (1918) time, not only in terms of institutional structure and governance but also its purpose in society. This is still the case a century later. Discussion is ongoing about the role of the university as a place of higher learning and/or vocational training. Corporations look to the university for academic and industrial innovation, scientific and technological advances, and the technical training needed in certain fields. In this regard, one measure of a university is how much it contributes to the economy, such as through training for certain fields of employment or the financial impact it has on the area where it is located (Aronowitz, 2000). Since the 1970s, there has been a greater emphasis on corporate research and employment-related education, a phenomenon advanced by corporate and government funding schemes that emphasize the sciences, health, and other areas that rely upon the infusion of university research and a supply of trained employees. The relationship between the university and corporate interests has been strengthened by private grant funding, and an even more intimate connection between the two is created when a university president joins a corporation's board of directors. Approximately half the presidents of the top forty research universities sit on at least one board (H. A. Giroux, 2014a, p. 59), further cementing the insider relationship between the corporation and the university. Funding from corporate donors puts the university and, through association, its faculty in curricular peril, as "officials scurry to forge alliances with large donors, offering to dedicate buildings and compromising chunks of the curriculum in return for financial support" (Aronowitz, 2000, p. 160). This tradeoff of programmatic decisions for financial gain may require faculty complicity, although the approval process does not require faculty approval.

There is also a significant relationship between universities and the US government. Even private universities receive a good deal of federal funding, although the nature of the research funded has changed in recent decades. Government entities such as the defense department and the National Science Foundation have funded a number of these institutions. Before 1980, much research was funded in theoretical areas of science such as physics and biology, even when there was no immediate economic use for the newly created knowledge (Aronowitz, 2000). In the post-Cold War era, the federal government's appetite for funding research without a utilitarian purpose declined precipitously; in other words, research considered less useful was less likely to be funded. Private research universities simultaneously came under federal scrutiny about how such public funds were used. As federal funding became more restricted, research universities began to enter into significant long-term funding arrangements with prosperous private corporations, such as Exxon, Monsanto, and DuPont (Aronowitz, 2000). Such fiduciary affiliations, whether between the university and the federal government or the university and private corporations, have put a particular burden on faculty scientists and researchers, who have largely become complicit as their work is increasingly funded by this revenue stream. With decreased government funding and the increased corporate influence that accompanies their financial investment, institutions are under pressure to make programmatic decisions based on external forces. As a result, the sciences that support corporate purposes have been favored, the humanities and cultural knowledge have suffered, and professional administrators of the financially driven university are looking for more flexibility (Aronowitz, 2000). Faculty have thus become something less than what they once were—experts in their fields who drove the creation of new knowledge. As power shifts further away from faculty and toward professional administrators, the university culture is increasingly corporatized, research and knowledge creation is further relegated to instrumental purposes, and, perhaps most critically, "the university intellectual is reduced to low level technocrat whose role is to manage and legitimate the downsizing, knowledge production, and labor practices that characterize the institutional power and culture of the corporatized and vocationalized university" (Giroux, 2011, p. 52). Research and writing are still an important element of faculty work, but they have become "increasingly instrumental to the overarching goal of individual survival, let alone advancement, in the academic hierarchy" (Aronowitz, 2000, p. 67). As a result, faculty members feel increasingly like employees who need to justify their existence to the university through grant writing, the production of knowledge considered useful to the corporate world, and other fiscally responsible activities. They have to a degree surrendered autonomy and retreated from being the academic intellectuals responsible for curriculum. In short, many faculty now feel resigned to being "transformed from a community of scholars to a collection of individual entrepreneurs" (Aronowitz, 2000, p. 164). Such resignation further advances the lessening in efforts and openness toward, and the precipitous decline in faculty engagement in shared governance.

A complete study of the modern university must understand not only the relationship between corporations and the university but that between the military and the university. Since World War I, the US military has looked to universities as drivers of scientific discovery and technological innovation. University research has led to the development of technological weapons such as the atomic bomb, and major research universities have arrangements for government funding through the US military. In January 1961, in his final speech before leaving office, President Eisenhower offered his much-quoted line warning of the "military-industrial complex," and of the danger of establishing too close a relationship between the military and the country's universities. What most do not know about this speech is that he warned in an earlier draft against creating a "military-industrial-academic complex," which noted the cozy relationship between the university system, the production of knowledge, and the purposes of the military system (Giroux, 2007). The federal government has since attempted to control the university as a space for research and the production of technological knowledge deemed useful in terms of making war, providing for the national defense, and strengthening homeland security. This now-normalized link—yet another blow to the institutional independence constitutive of shared governance—between the military and higher education is accepted by both liberals and conservatives (Giroux, 2007).

The Social and Democratic Purposes of Higher Learning

Finally, when considering the impact neoliberal policies have had on faculty participation in academic decision-making, reflection on the influence faculty should have on curriculum and programs is inevitable. Higher education, and particularly public higher education, must be considered a public good that is crucial to producing a citizenry capable of supporting democracy and social and democratic structures. This entails providing an education based on students' ability to question and critique all aspects of the world order. Enabling such a deep critique requires that faculty be free to explore democratic pedagogical practices that are based on an ecology of knowledges (Sousa Santos, 2014), equity, and justice. Developing this type of educational system first requires educators to be free to question and critique their own teaching and the system in which they work. To do this, educators must have a "vision of schooling as a democratic public sphere" (H. A. Giroux, 2014a, p. 39), with the understanding that this vision is not a method of instruction but a global educational project. Educators need to understand that their work on this project is a never-ending activity that must always be meaningful to students, one in which they see themselves as agents of the community with the goal of creating an environment in which students can become civically engaged. Through this kind of praxis, higher education faculty may regain agency in their own work while helping to create a movement to regain collective voice within the academy (H. A. Giroux, 2014a).

Indeed, it is precisely this characteristic of a vibrant democracy that is needed in the academy and that frightens corporate and government power: the democratic ideal of individual and collective voices, which allows for the critique of power as well as the potential fracture of dominant social norms. Social and political conservatives have charged colleges and universities with corrupting youth, claiming that the academy unduly prompts students to challenge traditional thinking on issues of race, gender, justice, and patriotism, and to freely and openly critique the dominant culture. They offer tradition as a counter to such a critique, even when tradition perpetuates racist stereotypes of people of African descent as something less than human and includes a reverence for a history that is bereft of the study of women (Nussbaum, 1998). The United States, more than any other nation, has attempted to extend higher education to all citizens, regardless of their race, class, or other identification. It also has articulated a unique commitment to higher learning not solely to prepare for a career but also to support citizenship and democratic social structures. However, this promise to educate all citizens and to educate for democracy has remained unfulfilled for many. Citizens marginalized by race, ethnicity, gender, class, and other non-dominant social classifications find that their own experiences and understanding of life are not valued within the dominant educational structure, and that in order to participate they must conform. As Nussbaum's writes, "They should not expect that their own experiences and traditions will form part of the curriculum. They may enter the academy only on sufferance and in disguise" (1998, p. 295). This describes the indoctrinating powers of the "melting pot" of American culture, a space of voluntary blindness where all are treated as members of one monolithic culture. According to Macedo (2009, p. 43), "the melting pot theory represents a second stage of quasi-genocide designed to enable the dominant cultural group to consolidate its cultural hegemony." While we may find isolated examples of a curriculum designed to advantage local cultures and knowledge, the dominant curricula and pedagogy continue to stress the vocational influence of a corporatized world, thereby perpetuating the hegemonic apparatus of higher education. The pretense is that curriculum and pedagogy are neutral and devoid of cultural influences, a claim that is in itself a political statement (Macedo, 2009). As its curricula become more vocationalized, the US higher education system is further selling short the democratic values and ideals so clearly held by many.

The corporatized university is not organized to offer time for contemplation and critique. Here, "Time refers not only to the way in which it is mediated differently by institutions, administrators, faculty, and students but also to how it shapes and allocates power, identities, and space through a particular set of codes and interests"

(Giroux, 2011, p. 113). Time governs not only the pace of work and decision-making but, perhaps more critically, the space allotted within the academy for such work, contemplation, and critique. In today's academic environment, public time has been decimated by the pervasive corporatization of institutional culture. Faculty are now confronted with the challenges of reestablishing public time in the form of a space for academic dialog and critique, and for a renewed sense of the faculty role in shared governance. None of this is easy to do, particularly with the radical transformation of the university over the past four decades—a transformation manufactured to attack higher learning as a seat of dissent—and university governance so dominated by professional administrators. Faculties have been split into competing and contrasting classifications, such as the divides between full-time and part-time and between the declining humanities and the technology fields privileged by industry. As an element of global neoliberalism, elites within and outside academia have chosen isolation as they seek to be separated from other elements of the population, while others frequently pay a heavy price for the newly created isolation of those privileged few (Bauman, 1998). All of these schisms and classifications breed resentment and animosity, and have nearly meant the demise

> of the university as a democratic public sphere. Many faculties are now demoralized as they increasingly lose rights and power . . . Demoralization often translates less into moral outrage than into cynicism, accommodation, and a retreat into a sterile form of professionalism.
>
> (H. A. Giroux, 2014a, p. 17)

This form of professionalism takes for granted the current hegemony of diminished faculty influence in higher education governance. Cynicism, while perhaps understandable, serves as a white flag of surrender from faculty to current-day professional administrators. It negates any opportunity for powerful critique, and further relegates governance to a cadre of professional administrators. Optimism and hope are foundational prerequisites for revitalizing shared governance. Hope is

> a referent for civic courage that translates as a political practice and begins when one's life can no longer be taken for granted, making concrete the possibility for transforming politics into an ethical space and a public act that confronts the flow of

everyday experience and the weight of social suffering with the force of individual and collective resistance and the unending project of democratic social transformation.

(H. A. Giroux, 2014a, p. 50)

This chapter has exposed the realities and contradictions of the new political economy of higher education. It has investigated past and current organizational structures, including the decline in number and change in status of the faculty-administrator, the similar trajectory of forms of shared governance, and the dramatic rise of professional management. It has described the increased corporate influence within US colleges and universities and how new corporate partnerships are influencing curriculum. Finally, it examined the historic and changing role higher education plays in readying citizens to participate in a vibrant social democracy. With these changes in mind, I will now focus on US community colleges. I will investigate the history of community colleges, their mission and purpose within the US higher education system, and the impact the neoliberal ideological framework has had on these institutions over the past four decades.

3 The New Political Economy of Community Colleges

In this chapter, I examine US community colleges, tracing their history from the early twentieth century through a number of transformations in mission and purpose. I scrutinize the unique characteristics of community colleges, including their ability to adapt quickly to governmental and/or corporate aims in changing circumstances. I investigate the historic and current-day connections between community colleges, the economy, and economic development, including the institution's role in workforce training programs and the associated vocationalization of its curriculum. This chapter extends the analysis of the previous chapter to include an interrogation of the role community college faculty play in academic decision-making at their institutions. Lastly, but importantly, I consider the question of who attends community colleges and the potential subalternization of certain populations to receive a different, more vocational education than others.

Junior colleges, now referred to as community colleges, have been part of the post-secondary education system in the United States for more than a century. Most educational historians credit Joliet Junior College, established in 1901 in Illinois' Joliet Township High School, with being the first US community college (Ayers et al., 2010). At the time, the junior college mission was focused on giving students a foundation for higher level studies and preparing them to transfer to baccalaureate-granting institutions. After completing their junior college studies, students at Joliet Junior College would transfer to a "senior" institution, such as the nearby University of Chicago, to earn a baccalaureate degree.

Throughout the next several decades, the junior college mission was transformed and broadened (Spielbauer, 2010). During the economic roar of the 1920s, industry wanted employees with more technical training. The need for workforce training grew significantly during the Great Depression, as the spurt of government public works projects called for more skilled workers. To satisfy this need, the US government became invested in creating more junior colleges, whose mission was to provide this workforce training (Spielbauer, 2010). During World War II, with the rapidly changing needs of wartime industry training, junior colleges gained a reputation for being flexible and able to adapt quickly to meet the demands of the volatile industrial environment. This ability to adjust quickly, to recalibrate to meet the educational and training needs of a changing society, has been an identifying trait of junior colleges ever since (Spielbauer, 2010). As World War II ended and soldiers were returning home, the nation's junior colleges filled the dual roles of retraining returning veterans for employment and equipping the academically under-prepared for future baccalaureate study, the latter of which was more in line with the original junior college mission (Spielbauer, 2010). During this time, junior colleges were increasingly referred to as community colleges, in no small part due to President Truman's Commission on Higher Education's endorsement of the name change. In a 1947 report entitled "Higher Education for American Democracy," the Commission envisioned a national system of community colleges that was free for all qualified students. It saw higher education as a significant factor in creating a free and democratic society (Ayers et al., 2010).

The name change from junior to community college, as well as the democratic purpose of higher education embraced by the Commission, showed like-minded support for the educational vision espoused three decades earlier by Dewey (2004). The name change paralleled Dewey's belief that a community sustains itself through education and that the educational process depends on the social environment in which the learner is engaged. It is precisely this connection between the learning environment and the learner's social engagement in their community that is at the heart of the belief that higher education can provide a significant source of support for a democratic society—what Dewey (2004) espouses as a critical component in learning. According to Dewey (2004, p. 95), a democratic society "must have a type of education which gives individuals a personal interest in social relationships and control." Further, "Knowledge that is worthy of being called knowledge, training of the intellect that is sure to amount to anything, is obtained only by participating intimately and actively in activities of social life" (Dewey & Dewey, 1915, p. 63). The student and the curriculum are powerful interrelated forces that interact with each other in their environment. The connection between the two, including the student's interaction with the social environment, is critically important to any meaningful learning process. It may be said that a student, by acting in the learning environment, learns by doing (Dewey & Dewey, 1915). This does not mean there is no instruction, but that the sources of information the student encounters are more varied:

> The teacher and the book are no longer the only instructors; the hands, the eyes, the ears, in fact the whole body, become sources of information, while teacher and text-book become respectively the starter and the tester. No book or map is a substitute for personal experience; they cannot take the place of the actual journey. The mathematical formula for a falling body does not take the place of throwing stones or shaking apples from a tree.
>
> (Dewey & Dewey, 1915, p. 74)

As we consider the educational process and the vital relationship between the learner and their social environment, it is also important to contemplate the relationship between work and education. Education is a social endeavor, as is work, particularly in an increasingly technological environment. Thus, a primary purpose of public education is to teach the student to live in and interact with their world (Dewey & Dewey, 1915). This includes making it possible to receive an education that gives the student a start in the world and enables them to engage in a variety of forms of work as social and industrial conditions change. Schools therefore must reject a uniform curriculum and focus on providing an education that addresses local interests, social conditions, and occupations (Dewey & Dewey, 1915, p. 205). Such an education will enhance the student's chances of leading a successful life in their social, work, and civic spheres. The education experience will thus impact not only students' own lives and the lives of their friends and family but their community, the "life of the locality" (Dewey & Dewey, 1915, p. 206).

As scientific and technological advances have impacted industry and society, social and political forces have become increasingly bound to the economic. This demands an examination of how the social activity of education has been affected by these changing dynamics. Public schooling in the United States began at a time when industry was less important, "when there was no positive connection between science and the operations of production and distribution of goods" (Dewey & Dewey, 1915, p. 229). Since that time, the relationship between public schooling and employment has changed dramatically, which is illustrated by an etymological study of the word "school," which derives from the Greek word for "leisure" and thus signifies a historic division between the working class and the leisure class. In feudal societies, work done by hand was carried out by a socially inferior, oppressed class: "Training for them was a servile sort of education, while *liberal* education was an education for a free man, and a free man was a member of the upper classes" (Dewey & Dewey, 1915, p. 231). While much has changed since feudal times, there is an eerie similarity between the conditions of that era and the current relationship between the opportunities for a liberal education and an education focused on training for employable skills, as well as the social class positions of the citizens who engage in these varied forms of education. As this chapter progresses, we will revisit this notion as we discuss the diverse characteristics of community college students.

The postwar expansion of community colleges in the United States, which got a boost from the Truman Commission's recognition that community colleges were a compelling public good, was greatly enhanced by the GI Bill of Rights, which provided government financial support to returning veterans attending college (Spielbauer, 2010). The tremendous expansion of community colleges in the United States during the Cold War years of the 1950s and 1960s involved both the number of institutions and the scope of their mission. The community college mission of baccalaureate transfer and industry training remained the same, but these institutions became increasingly invested in their local communities and provided ever more services to a broader populace (Ward, 2001). In addition to open door policies that allowed more people to work toward a baccalaureate degree, community colleges offered a wide array of educational programs at a relatively low cost. Over the decades, many political and business leaders pushed for a more narrow focus on granting vocational degrees, yet, by the 1970s, community colleges had begun to offer a wide variety of services and programs, such as developmental education, academic and career advising, vocational education, education for transfer and the liberal arts, and an increasing connection to their communities. However, the main purpose of the community college remained to provide a path toward baccalaureate transfer (Ayers et al., 2010).

Over the past four decades, there has been a significant shift in the focus of the community college mission. The dominant national view is no longer congruent with that espoused by the Truman Commission, that the role of public higher education is to contribute to a "free and democratic society." Current government policy stresses workforce training, thus inextricably linking the community college curriculum to developing workforce skills, as dictated by industry (Ayers et al., 2010). Aronowitz (2013) argues that this alignment of higher education with workforce training is ironic because full-time employment is becoming less abundant. So, while higher education moves toward a corporate workforce training model and employability standards, the opportunities for employment leading to a career are decreasing. Nevertheless, the realignment toward corporate training in higher education is true not only of community colleges but of all of higher education, which has been realigned to serve the corporate economy. Instead of serving the common good, as espoused by the Truman Commission, higher education has increasingly become an instrument of the corporate elite (Giroux, 2011).

By definition and mission, community colleges have close ties to the community, including local industry and corporations. Industry looks to community colleges to provide the local workforce with the skills, training, and other attributes it requires. However, Nussbaum (2010) charges that, by focusing on the specific technical job skills some employers seek, community colleges deprive their students of a chance to learn the skills most employers really want in their employees. She argues that a decreased emphasis on education in the humanities is rampant throughout the world and that it is actually hurting economic development. Nussbaum contends that the so-called "soft" skills of a liberal education, such as the ability to adapt, think critically, and communicate, are vitally important to employment in the continually changing technological world, more so than technical training for a specific job that may require very different skills in the future. Nussbaum (2010) also argues that the skills associated with a liberal education foster support for community and democratic organizations, which are the attributes of higher education espoused by the Truman Commission. The constitution of higher education, and more specifically the character of the US community college, has strayed far from this mission in various ways. In addition to the negative impact a reduced focus on liberal arts and the humanities has on students, the new managerialism of neoliberal education policy (Lynch, 2014) has largely removed the democratic process from academic decision-making, including the faculty role in that process (Levin, Kater, & Wagoner, 2006).

This has hastened a change in focus away from the critical thinking skills employers say they want toward low-level, middle-skilled employment training. The resultant short-term, technical skills do not foster the essential abilities students must develop to communicate, think, adapt, and engage, not only in employment but in taking part in a truly democratic society. A society lacking such skills and abilities will move ever farther away from the US ideal of participation in a "thick democracy" (Gandin & Apple, 2002), one based on inclusion and authentic participation.

The Vocationalization of Community Colleges

What constitutes a successful higher education? For years before neoliberal ideology became dominant, the ideological trend which prevailed in public opinion was generally in line with the Commission on Higher Education's statement that the mission of higher education was to support a democratic society (Schrum, 2007). That view no longer prevails and in fact might appear quaint or even misguided. Corporate pressure for workforce training has led to changes in the curriculum and pedagogy at all levels, but perhaps most notably at community colleges, where faculty have become increasingly engaged in corporate training. This involves teaching specific technical skills for middle-skilled employment, jobs that require some postsecondary education but not a baccalaureate degree. Curriculum is often designed to meet specific industry needs, and even desired educational outcomes, traditionally the purview of faculty, may be dictated by industry (Wilson, 2010). The changes in curricular focus at community colleges are made more problematic by the fact that the faculty are predominantly part-time employees who are working for low pay in a highly structured environment. Whether full- or part-time, however, many community college faculty have increasingly become "agents of a corporate ideology that arguably makes them instruments and not autonomous professionals" (Levin et al., 2006, p. 3). The vocationalization of the community college curriculum is also problematic because it has occurred at the expense of the study of humanities and the arts—precisely the areas of study that foster creativity, imagination, and the social and critical thinking skills needed to support democratic institutions. It is important to point out that these are the very skills most employers want—the ability to be flexible and to adapt in an ever-changing global job market (Nussbaum, 2010).

This situation is further complicated by the fact that curricular changes have been made in response not only to corporate desires, and often the stated needs of local community industries, but also to the desires of students and parents. Students who come to college looking for job skills fail to understand that the skills and training that may help them get immediate employment may not serve them well in the dynamic global economy (Ginsberg, 2011), in life, or in their social and political participation (K. Saltman, personal communication, March 6, 2015). Parents also complicate matters when they look for a financial return on their tuition dollars in the form of preparing their child for future employment (Ginsberg, 2011), a tendency that occurs across all segments of higher education. This is a clear indication of how market fundamentalism has saturated our personal, professional, and social lives with the notion that education and employment training are one and the same. To wit, "Neoliberalism appears in the now commonsense framing of education exclusively through presumed ideals of upward individual economic mobility (the promise of cashing in knowledge for jobs)" (Saltman, 2012, p. 98). In both instances, education and employment training, the pervasive influence of the modern-day job market leads people and institutions to make important long-term decisions about the direction of education based on a short-term vision that is often dictated by industry. These decisions have transformed institutions, most notably community colleges, from centers focused on the creativity and critical thinking of higher learning to "knowledge factories," centers of vocational training that prepare students for low-paid, low-skilled employment—in essence, preparing them to "take their places as subprofessionals in the increasingly volatile technoscientific industries" (Aronowitz, 2000, p. 56).

There has been a close relationship for generations between higher education and the economy. Research conducted at higher education institutions leads to new knowledge and technologies, which has an impact on both industry and the economy. As described earlier, community colleges have long been engaged in providing education and training that support new and changing industries, and they are increasingly viewed as an important asset for economic development across the country (Jacobs, 2012). A generation ago, economic development focused on physical and political factors that supported economic activity, such as transportation, tax policies, and proximity to major research universities, which attracted businesses to areas where economic conditions were favorable. While these factors are still present today, as "industries became more complex and knowledge-driven, this approach to economic development began to evolve, and the skills of workers at all levels of production and development needed to be enhanced" (Jacobs, 2012, p. 193). This recent emphasis on the human resources needed for both innovation and production has been a significant change. Employees at all levels of industry are now expected to have the skills and knowledge not only to do their specific job but to adjust to changing technologies and take advantage of the technological advances in their industry.

An interesting assertion can be made about this process. Community colleges will clearly continue to provide workforce training, but a strong argument can be made that the original mission of the community college—to prepare students to transfer to institutions offering baccalaureate degrees—and its liberal arts foundation must remain vital components of the community college education. The flexibility needed in the modern workforce and the increasing need for more education, including baccalaureate study, demand the retention of these components. In the current environment, there is a significant desire to connect community colleges even more closely to the education and training needs of industry, and thus to produce potential employees who have both the ability to think critically and the specific job skills necessary to adapt in an ever-changing technological environment (Jacobs, 2012).

Circumstances in recent years have provided yet another compelling force to cement the role of the community college as a key driver of workforce preparation. These forces connect community colleges to the business world not only by providing skilled technicians but also through local entrepreneurial activities. Numerous institutions have created close working relationships with economic development actors in their areas, which means that "community colleges can play a role in the actual formation of companies through a business incubator approach" (Jacobs, 2012, p. 198). This particular type of relationship between industry and the community college signifies yet another potential major change in the US higher education mission and purpose.

The increased connection between higher learning and the economy is a signal that we have entered a time of economic crisis in which rampant forces of production and exchange will cause periodic deflation (Marx & Bender, 2013). Society today is so consumed with the search for unending profit that it has created an "epidemic of over-production," a state of economic starvation in which all means of sustenance have been depressed, where "there is too much civilisation, too much means of subsistence, too much industry, too much commerce" (Marx & Bender, 2013, p. 66). These elements of society may seem incongruous: why would more production, more commerce, and more exchange not lead to further expansion, a burgeoning economy, society, and middle class? The answer may appear as simple as the question: the productive forces have become too powerful for the societal conditions in which they have been created. As modes of production outpace the conditions they were intended to serve, they create disorder. A "society that has conjured up such gigantic means of production and of exchange, is like the sorcerer, who is no longer able to control the powers of the nether world whom he has called up by his spells" (Marx & Bender, 2013, p. 66). We now find ourselves in such circumstances—with stifling production and exchange that have outpaced the economy. Universities and community colleges exist, and are immersed, in an environment of such crises.

US higher education and community colleges are prime examples of this over-production: they are producing a glut of PhDs who are unable to find full-time employment in higher education and at the same time are pushed to produce more graduates. The conditions of current society are simply "too narrow to comprise the wealth created by them," yet the solution will mandate a further exploitation of existing markets and the creation of new ones—in other words, the solution will involve "paving the way for more extensive and more destructive crises, and by diminishing the means whereby crises are prevented" (Marx & Bender, 2013, p. 67).

In this environment, the close ties between community colleges and local industry have in many instances fostered a curricular connection between the college's and corporate interests. Some have charged that corporate involvement in planning the community college curriculum has altered the faculty's role and narrowed the scope of what they teach (Wilson, 2010). In fact, determining the knowledge, skills, and abilities graduates need is increasingly influenced by industry. Representatives from local companies often team with community college faculty to develop academic and training programs (Wilson, 2010). As such, faculty are designing the curriculum around what industry believes students need to be prepared for the workforce.

The issue of incorporating technical training into mainstream education is a longstanding concern. In his later years, W. E. B. DuBois feared the advance of the technical side of academia and warned against the bifurcation of education—on the one hand, providing students with the technical training required for specific employment and, on the other, providing a broad education suitable for further study (S. S. Giroux, 2014). This reciprocal relationship between corporate and academic entities is currently not only accepted by many community college educators, but it is also lauded as a best practice. According to Wilson (2010, p. 9), a North Carolina community college president boasts that

> employers come up with the baseline—what they want students to do—and the faculty takes that and develops the curriculum . . . The beauty of it is that the companies have bought into the process, they have ownership of this, and they support the program.

While accepted by many, this practice may be damaging, not only to community colleges' curricular offerings and the students they serve but also to the professionalism of community college faculty. In designing and delivering a curriculum deemed important by industry, community college faculty may no longer be seen as the curricular experts in their fields, but instead be relegated to a more technical role, acting less as curriculum designers than as translators of industry's needs into instructional strategies (Wilson, 2010). This represents a downgrading of community college faculties' professional status and is an extreme example of Freire's (2000) banking concept of education, whereby knowledge is bestowed by those who are knowledgeable on those who know nothing. The process projects "absolute ignorance onto others, a characteristic of the ideology of oppression, negates education and knowledge as processes of inquiry" (Freire, 2000, p. 72). The evidence is clear that, while it differs in impact in various regions and institutions, corporate influence on the community college curriculum is a reality.

While Ayers et al. (2010), Wilson (2010), Levin et al. (2006), and others point to these problems at community colleges, Giroux (2011), Aronowitz (2000), Ginsberg (2011), Slaughter and Rhoades (2004), and Nussbaum (2010) point to a shift in focus in the entire higher education system, where the curriculum is increasingly stripped of its historical devotion to critical thinking, writing, teaching, and learning. Even university curricula are increasingly focused on technical training at the command of corporate entities. This devotion to the influence of the global market has transformed all of higher education into a tool of the corporate world, "shifting power away from faculty to administrations, and corporatizing the culture of the university" (Giroux, 2011, p. 52). Giroux further charges that "the university intellectual is reduced to low-level technocrat whose role is to manage and legitimate the downsizing, knowledge production, and labor practices that characterize the institutional power and culture of the corporatized and vocationalized university" (Giroux, 2011, p. 52), signifying another step toward implementation of the neoliberal agenda as related to the downgrading of faculty status as being an integral component of institutional governance.

Joining Ayers et al. (2010), Wilson (2010), Giroux (2011), Nussbaum (2010), and others in warning of the dangers of the corporatization of higher education and the associated shift away from education's support of democratic structures, John Curtis of the American Association of University Professors says that, as community college curriculum becomes more corporatized,

> it's sometimes difficult to convince students—and their parents, and legislators—that it's more important for them to get an education than to find the quickest route to a job. But if students can learn to think for themselves and confront new ideas critically, they won't have to go back and get retrained for a new job every four years—and they'll be better prepared as citizens in the process.
>
> (Wilson, 2010, p. 10)

The dramatic impact of these shifts in academic focus is significant not only for colleges and universities but for the students and educators who, if these shifts are not reconsidered and altered, will be educated and will educate within the hegemony of an efficient and corporatized educational model (Wilson, 2010).

Technology and labor have been intimately connected since the Industrial Age, and this is still the case today. At the same time, employers, including community colleges, are no longer as committed as they historically were to providing full-time employment and a career path with upward mobility (Aronowitz, 2013). The advances in technology and the resultant shrinking of the world have led to job losses and a changing work environment. There is still sufficient work, but it is increasingly being done by part-time, contingent workers. Even in higher education, where there is still a semblance of full-time employability, only 27 percent of all faculty have full-time employment (Aronowitz, 2013). Similar to the extreme example, given in Chapter 2, of the almost exclusive use of part-time faculty at Southern New Hampshire University's College of Online and Continuing Education, in the neighboring state of Vermont, there is an even more extreme example in the community college realm. The Community College of Vermont (CCV), constituted of a statewide system of publically supported institutions, relies on the exclusive use of part-time faculty. In addition to the cost-savings associated with having no full-time faculty, the system also owns no property (Tollefson, Garrett, & Ingram, 1999). The CCV policy of hiring only part-time faculty has allowed for an expansion of the college's administration, while relegating its faculty to struggle for financial survival (Brunton, 2016). Even as they work beyond their teaching responsibilities, participating on committees, and dedicating themselves to the success of their students and the mission of the college, CCV faculty have no job security, no retirement plan, no health insurance, and no contingency for missing work due to illness. Such circumstances have consigned these highly educated and dedicated professionals to a condition of employment which holds no hope for advancement, and no hope to earn a living wage, as a CCV faculty member (Brunton, 2016).

In the current political economy, which is based on neoliberal ideology, community colleges have adjusted to changing corporate demands with workforce training programs and by contracting to provide short-term, specialized skills training. They also have changed their academic curricula to focus on what some see as "employability" skills (Levin et al., 2006). With community colleges being truly local and of the community, including the business community and government entities that provide their base funding, they have become ever more closely linked to a system of economic globalization. With their emphasis on workforce-related education and training for local markets, and their dependence on local government for the resources needed to operate, community colleges have become an economic implement in the global economy. By increasingly providing workforce training in specific skills, rather than a broad and critically transforming education, community colleges are progressively transferring onto their students Bauman's (1998) status of being a "local" citizen—one who is trapped in a globalized reality, incapable of experiencing the full breadth of the world.

Paving the Way for Venture Capitalism

Nationwide, state commitment to public higher education has been unraveling for many years (Couturier, 2005). This has been reflected in significant decreases in state funding for public higher education, which has had a great impact on community colleges and their ability to effectively serve their communities, individual students, and area businesses. In the five fiscal years from 2009 to 2014, state funding for public higher education was reduced in thirty-one of the fifty states (Center for the Study of Education Policy, 2015).

Public colleges and universities have reacted to reduced government funding by seeking other sources of revenue, such as public and private grants and philanthropic donations. While these efforts have been relatively successful, they have changed the nature of both administration and faculty roles; many academic professionals are now evaluated and rewarded based on their ability to secure grant funding (H. A. Giroux, 2014a). Moreover, public and private institutions are often expected to fulfil certain conditions and expectations laid out by those who provide their funding (Boyd, 2011). This situation calls into question the motives and identities of those who are making funding decisions for these institutions.

Colleges and universities in fact have a long history of raising money from external sources, both public and private, including grants from public entities like the National Science Foundation, from private sources such as the Lumina Foundation, and from local, regional, and national philanthropic organizations. Philanthropic organizations and individuals have a significant history of giving to higher education institutions. Numerous nineteenth- and twentieth-century industrialists and financiers endowed charitable foundations, notably the Carnegie, Ford, and Rockefeller foundations. This philanthropy flowed from fortunes accumulated by extracting profits from the control of economic markets, in most cases before financial markets were regulated (Lewis, 1963). Most captains of industry saw philanthropy as a way to create a legacy and extend the life of their family name. In many cases, it put the family name in a more favorable light than may have been the case while a given family was actively accumulating its wealth (Lewis, 1963). Some donors, including Carnegie, Ford, and Rockefeller, also viewed philanthropy as a public obligation, a way of giving back some of their good fortune. This "scientific philanthropy" meant gifts were granted to educational institutions without any preconditions or directions on how to use the funds (Saltman, 2010).

During the past four decades of market fundamentalism, there have been dramatic changes in philanthropic giving within both

K-12 and higher education. In addition to there being new and different family names—such as Broad, Gates, and Walton—behind the foundations, the new philanthropists have a clear political agenda: the application of neoliberal policies to public institutions. Another critical difference lies in the fact that a donation from a foundation today is less a gift than an investment in the institution, one that carries the expected return of promoting neoliberal policies (Saltman, 2010). This new philanthropy is based on the market activity of venture capitalism, where investors contribute their money but want to see a return on their investment; in the education context, returns sometimes materialize in the form of a financial profit and sometimes in a shift toward market-based educational policy. Coined "venture philanthropy" (Saltman, 2010, p. 1), this new form of giving supports the further infusion of market fundamentalism into public education. This includes the conception of public schooling as a developing private market for the purpose of private capital's extraction of public dollars for private gain.

Venture philanthropy provides funding for an educational institution or system of institutions at the cost of promoting policies that further privatize and deregulate public education. Venture philanthropy promotes market-driven policies like those in which certain public services must be paid for by the public, or in which teachers and students are paid for test results (Saltman, 2010). Its actors have blurred the public/private divide by bringing complex motives and values to education funding. As such, "privatization as a material and discursive process is partial and very diverse, sometimes faltering but of massive and increasing importance within and over and against public sector education" (Ball, 2007, p. 134). While providing much-needed funding, venture philanthropy money is not a gift but an investment, replete with demands and limitations that give the donor undue influence and affect the institution's educational practices and policies, including governance (Ball, 2007).

Venture philanthropy provides only a small fraction of education funding, but it can wield great influence over a wide variety of institutional policies and procedures, including those related to finance, curriculum, and pedagogy. It also employs business models for educational purposes and uses business jargon which is now taken for granted in educational contexts—terms such as efficiency, accountability, leveraging, bringing to scale—to influence the structural ethos of the institution, while also labeling schools and their programs, teachers, and students as underperformers, or even failures. Such "market metaphors stand in for evidence of meaningful educational improvements while making privatization and deregulation seem naturally beneficial by associating them with the unquestioned superiority of business practices" (Saltman, 2010, p. 5). Perhaps, the most insidious unseen danger of venture philanthropy is the accountability measures that take control out of the hands of educators and place it squarely in the hands of industrialists, financiers, and the financial corporate elite. While no measures of educational quality are beyond scrutiny and no educational system should be regarded as better than all others, consider the example of Finland, a country widely recognized as having one of the top elementary and secondary school systems in the world, as measured by standardized tests. According to Sahlberg (2011), nowhere in the Finnish education system can you find the word "accountability." Meanwhile, although they are known to cause damage to students, curriculum, pedagogy, and teachers, measures of accountability are at the core of neoliberal educational policies and a foundational basis of much of venture philanthropy. While represented in the media as selfless generosity, venture philanthropy is in fact an investment, both social and financial, in supplanting the voices of educators with the voices of the corporate elite (Saltman, 2010).

None of this is to suggest, of course, that there is no longer any philanthropic giving not characterized as venture philanthropy. The point here is to identify venture philanthropy as a new form of "strings-attached" philanthropy that closely resembles venture capitalism, often includes ideological conditions, and seeks to influence policy. So, while true philanthropic activity in the model of Carnegie, Ford, and Rockefeller may still exist, the new form of philanthropic endeavor in the venture philanthropy era— represented by investors such as the Broad, Gates, and Walton foundations—carries the expectation that their generosity allows business professionals to influence education policy, thereby furthering the neoliberal agenda.

To adjust to this challenging and changing environment and to meet its financial needs, the community college has developed an entrepreneurial culture in which the economic goals of production, efficiency, and generating new sources of funding now occupy a major place in the institutional mission. Consistent with this corporate mentality, the community college has moved to a model that relies on more part-time labor, in line with the overall trend in the industrialized economy (Levin et al., 2006). Some institutions have been more successful than others in transitioning to this corporate educational ethos. Those resilient enough to thrive in this new economy have exhibited the ability to adapt to the changing political, technological, and economic conditions of their existence. In fact, many community colleges have proven to be flexible, responsive, and able to serve a multitude of functions for many constituencies. Among their varied roles and responsibilities include providing services for English language learners and workforce training for displaced and under-employed workers, as well as continuing their traditional role of preparing students to transfer to baccalaureate programs. Providing all these varied services with reduced public funding has stretched community colleges very thin. This affects their ability to provide the type of education worthy of the ideals of many community college educators, such as a broad curriculum, range of services, and quality instruction (Levin et al., 2006). The adaptability and nimbleness of US community colleges in terms of developing new curriculum and instructional methodologies is a feature that dates back to the mid-twentieth century (Spielbauer, 2010). While this flexibility continues to be an asset, it also has challenged and altered the nature of work within the institution. Increased government use of community colleges to address workforce needs, without any commensurate increase in funding, has both created significant managerial pressures and "framed the identity of community colleges as economic institutions" (Levin et al., 2006, p. 8).

Complicating matters further, the community college student population is also rapidly changing. Access to education and training has long been associated with a community college education (Spielbauer, 2010), and the institution today is increasingly emphasizing "access" to increase enrollments. Therefore, the nature of the teaching provided has changed to accommodate a wider range of student educational needs and interests. Community colleges and other institutions now openly profess to being "enrollment driven" as a way of competing for students, whose tuition dollars help institutions meet their financial needs. This enrollment-driven aspect impacts the nature of the community college, along with its faculty and the nature of their work (Levin et al., 2006). To survive in this changing environment, college presidents and administrations increasingly embrace a corporate ideology, connecting the work of education to the global economy. In fact, in many colleges and universities, the college president is now often referred to as the chief executive officer, further blurring the line between being an academic institution and a corporate entity (H. A. Giroux, 2014a).

Given the decrease in government funding and the need to raise funds elsewhere to survive, the US community college is seen as "progressively adopting the ideology of a corporation, assuming the identity of a business, and defining its core workforce—the faculty—as industrial or business labor, in line with the ideology of neo-liberalism" (Levin et al., 2006, p. 7). Faculty are increasingly viewed as a commodity, part of the corporate workforce, which frequently puts them in contradicting positions: they may state their opposition to the corporate community college model, yet at the same time support their institution in ways that conflict with their personal notion of what a college education should be. Whether or not they are aware of this potential conflict, faculty are often positioned to be developers, facilitators, and supporters of institutional corporate policy. This puts some of them in the demoralizing position of engaging in work that conflicts with their values, their educational philosophy being at odds with the institutional policies, methods, and programs that they support and promote. In this regard, faculty members may be agents of a philosophy they oppose, which, for some, may create deep personal conflict, including an awareness of oppression. Educators working within this culture of conflict rely on a "self-imposed censorship, so that the undesirable features of the organization and work are either eliminated or ignored" (Levin et al., 2006, p. 2).

According to H. A. Giroux (2014b), "the university has become an adjunct of corporate power." Many universities are complicit in this role. There is tremendous pressure on faculty—no longer just pressure to publish and be a public intellectual but to write grants, which for many is a mandate if they wish to earn tenure and remain employed. Giroux argues that grant-writing should not be confused with the acts of educating and engaging in academic discourse, contending, in addition, that "When intellectuals are reduced to grant writers—there is a violence there" (H. A. Giroux, 2014b). Reliance on grant monies has taken on such importance and is now so fully a part of academic culture that some faculty list the dollar amounts they have been awarded on their curriculum vitae as a sign of their transactional value in the hegemony of neoliberalism.

The work of community college faculty, who represent one-third of all US higher education faculty, is heavily impacted by neoliberal practices operating in conjunction with economic globalization.

Such faculty are predominantly part-time employees who work for low pay, get few benefits, and often have little to no job security (Levin et al., 2006). Combined with the fact that they often work in a highly structured environment, community college faculty have arguably become less than autonomous professionals, a situation compounded by the close relationship between community colleges and corporate partners. Faculty often serve in roles that support corporate interests, in a sense making them instruments of corporate purpose, although many do not see themselves in this light. They believe in the community college mission and see the college's open enrollment policy as a mechanism of social justice. Some believe this perspective has, in effect, tricked community college educators into docility, while rendering them complicit in the industrial influence on community college curricular offerings, since "The democratic and idealistic attributes of the community college—social mobility, open access, remediation—are the foundation for a corporate ethos which draws in and holds organizational members captive" (Levin et al., 2006, p. 8). This has allowed some institutions to justify their actions by citing their service to community, arguing that the social justice benefits gained in extending the ability for all to improve their lot in life and experience economic gain are goals worthy of pursuing at any cost. These goals have enabled community colleges to expand enrollments and increase revenues, which has also increased their reliance on part-time faculty (Boyd, 2011). This is now considered a permanent reliance wherein part-time faculty are no longer viewed as contingent faculty, a temporary part of the workforce, but are instead now part of a fully "institutionalized . . . [and] highly managed workforce as a result of the globalization of the community college." Although the policies that result in such use of faculty are framed as necessary in order to better serve community college students, this increased use of part-time faculty is in fact a tool to "achieve increased productivity and efficiency, and not to enhance student learning" (Levin et al., 2006, p. 12).

Technology, too, is having a significant impact on education in a variety of ways. Community colleges use new technologies to pursue their mission, particularly in providing access to higher education. As competition for tuition dollars continues to increase, colleges and universities are competing for the growing pool of potential students using online education. Online courses are increasingly popular, but they have limitations and the technologies they use are significantly restructuring faculty work (Levin et al., 2006). According to Aronowitz (2013), online coursework is "bereft of gesture," as teachers are not able to see if someone is "slumping in their seat" or has "excitement in their eyes." Moreover, online communications are less able to accommodate the active give and take of thorough dialog. Aronowitz also charges that the organizational structure of many online courses relies on students responding on command to a prompt. In this way, he suggests that technology has moved higher education closer to Skinner's behaviorist model, which invites conformity and a lack of critical thinking. However, not all faculty agree with Aronowitz, and many are eager to incorporate technology into their curriculum and instruction, and to engage in teaching online courses. This may also include faculty, whether in unionized or non-unionized environments, who are eager to expand employment opportunities. Even in unionized environments, through collective bargaining, they are party to the creation of policies intended to increase productivity and develop efficiencies, all of which helps to further establish an economic ethos within their institutions, developing a more dominant focus on the practicality as opposed to the effectiveness of institutional operations (Levin et al.)

With so many academic decisions being made by and for economic interests, reinserting an academic voice in higher education decision-making offers an opportunity to counter neoliberal policies. Moreover, faculty involvement in decision-making is a measure of their ability to impact educational policy (H. A. Giroux, 2014a). Understanding the dynamics of faculty involvement, or lack of involvement, in academic decision-making may lead to institutional decisions based on educational reasoning rather than market-based objectives. Some may argue that when faculty are placed in management roles, such as those of department chair or program coordinator, this offers an opportunity to engage academic intellectuals in managerial decisions. Others may be less optimistic, believing that the role of full-time faculty is central to the community college shift to a corporate model. According to Levin et al. (2006), full-time faculty do participate in managerial work, but their impact on substantial decision-making—such as determining policy—is minimal. In addition, with the increasing use of part-time faculty, who have historically had more limited roles and responsibilities in institutional governance, Levin et al. argue that the role, and workload, of full-time faculty has increased. In this context, full-time faculty—who are significantly outnumbered by part-timers—take on other significant duties, frequently in the name of shared governance; in fact, "As resources decline in public institutions of higher education, an emerging commodity available to management in exchange for increased production by faculty may be participation in decision-making" (Levin et al., 2006, p. 9). Still, the US community college system is not monolithic, and the roles and responsibilities of full-time and part-time faculty vary widely. Some institutions rely more heavily on part-time faculty who may be engaged to a greater extent in institutional governance structures, such as committee work, accreditation efforts, and program coordination. No matter the circumstance, examining the real impact of faculty on institutional governance is vitally important.

Community colleges are increasingly incorporating new management structures based on market ideology. Although management historically has exchanged faculty productivity for monetary rewards, there is a growing trend of exchanging participation in governance for productivity (Levin et al., 2006). This practice is, however, not completely new: paraphrasing Donald E. Walker, president of Southeastern Massachusetts University from 1972 to 1984, "When you don't have money to bargain, bargain away management rights" (C. Barrow, personal communication, March 24, 2014). This process of managing higher education through the exchange of goods (shared governance) and services (management productivity) is a classic example of neoliberal ideology, in which, "[b]y viewing shared governance not only as an academic tradition but also as an exchange of goods and services, we suggest a perspective indicative of the commodification of cooperation" (Levin et al., 2006, p. 9). This reconceptualization of shared governance has implications for institutional management and for faculty, relative to the mission of the institution. Legal language in collective bargaining agreements increasingly refers to exchanging participation in governance for an increased faculty workload, or perhaps a smaller salary increase, which formalizes the commodification of cooperation within institutional structures. This agreement to bargain cooperation and governance in community colleges suggests a fundamentally changing role for community college faculty, one which intertwines the traditional roles of faculty and management. This arrangement engages faculty in management while avoiding an associated engagement in the decision-making which determines the fundamental academic and curricular paths of the institution. In their expanding role as managers, faculty are viewed by administrators as "extensions of management and as contributors to the corporate strategies and goals of the institution" (Levin et al., 2006, p. 12). Even though they are involved and supporting such policies and actions, faculty are often marginalized in decision-making about institutional direction. Although faculty see themselves as central to the institution and actively participate in its administration and management, they remain on the periphery of decision-making because they work within a system that is focused on the concept of efficiency. In education, one strives to be both effective and efficient, whereas in a market economy, efficiency is the more highly valued goal. This conflict is not unique to community colleges, but with the increased emphasis in recent years on their economic goals, these institutions now tend to value productivity and efficiency.

The purpose of this book is less to provide a list of specific solutions, than it is to engage in a dialog of interrelated issues and ideas. While this dialog may lead to solutions, it is not my intent to profess them. Having said that, as we consider faculty voice and participation in institutional governance, there is a potential and a link that is worth noting, mainly, faculty unionism. The ideal of faculty engagement in decision-making is not represented by special interests and individual enterprise, but by collective and institutional activity, and commitment. As such, it is difficult to discuss collective engagement and voice of faculty without consideration of analogous forms of faculty unionism, including elements of social movement unionism, and autonomous collective faculty organizations such as faculty senates. While faculty unionism is beyond the scope of this book, and likely deserves the sole attention of another study, it should be expected that faculty voice and faculty unionism are inextricably linked and that this link may serve a useful part of further dialog.

Recent US presidents have aligned community colleges and workforce training. A significant example is President George W. Bush's Community College Initiative, which was administered not by the Department of Education but by the Department of Labor (Ayers et al., 2010). This trend of aligning community college policy with economic policy, rather than education policy, cannot be attributed to one presidential administration or one political party. According to President Obama,

> In the coming years, jobs requiring at least an associate degree are projected to grow twice as fast as jobs requiring no college experience. We will not fill those jobs—or keep those jobs on our shores—without the training offered by community colleges.
>
> (White House Website, 2014)

In addition to strengthening the hegemonic bond between a community college education and job training, the Obama administration continued the Bush administration practice of administering government programs for community colleges from the Department of Labor. On the community college page of the White House Website (2014), the Obama administration announced that $2 billion had been allocated to allow community colleges to offer "career training." The initiative, which is "housed at the Department of Labor and implemented in close cooperation with the Department of Education," offers community colleges the opportunity to "build partnerships with businesses and the workforce investment system" and "work closely with employers to design training that is relevant to the local labor market and likely to lead to employment and careers" (White House Website, 2014). Furthermore, there were just two links on the Higher Education page of the Obama White House website, under the heading "Strengthening Community Colleges": "Promoting Industry Partnerships to Foster Career Readiness" and "2 Million Jobs for Trained Workers" (White House Website, 2014). These examples demonstrate the essential connection between US community colleges and workforce training as defined by the Obama administration. Given this focus on the part of the federal government, the vulnerability of community colleges to the ideological agendas of venture philanthropy, whether funded by public or private sources, is clear.

The Subalternization of Community College Students and Faculties

In recent years, higher education has shifted its focus away from the critical thinking and inquiry associated with the humanities and the arts, including engagement in public activity that supports a free and democratic society, and toward specific technical training related to employability skills (Aronowitz, 2013; Giroux, 2011; Nussbaum, 2010). A significant problem that emerges from the latter sort of training is that students miss out on developing some of the most important skills and attributes their future employers will want—the so-called "soft" skills of a liberal education, such as the ability to write, speak to an audience, think critically, and adapt to a rapidly changing world and global market (Nussbaum, 2010). These attributes are vitally important for successful employment in the continually evolving technological world, much more so than technical training for a current job that may not require the same skills in future years.

This turn away from the humanities and toward training in specific technologies is a significant change in the way higher education operates, and, according to Nussbaum (2010), is actually hurting economic development. Moreover, the skills and attributes so important to the future workforce are also vitally important to the development of future civic and economic leaders—those who will govern their communities while supporting democracy and democratic institutions. These abilities are associated with achieving a well-rounded education and have been at the core of higher education for many decades, and ensuring their availability should remain in the domain of curricular experts (Ortega, 1944). However, the changes in focus at community colleges have brought a crucial loss of faculty control over curriculum content. Community colleges across the country have joined with corporate partners and venture philanthropists, supported by federal policy, who now determine the skills they want in a well-trained workforce. In this new economy of community college education, the faculty role is increasingly reduced to developing and delivering curriculum that satisfies these industry demands (Wilson, 2010). Community college faculty have become progressively marginalized and are recognized today less as curricular experts and increasingly as purveyors of information and training, those who translate industry needs into curricular and instructional strategies—in short, those who provide workforce skills (Wilson, 2010). This changing role calls into question the very nature of the community college faculty, as faculty members are losing both the distinction of being the experts in their academic fields and the ability to shape the curricula of their institutions.

Accepting that there is "mission differentiation" among the different sectors of higher education and that community colleges are under significant pressure to provide an education that leads to specific technical employment opportunities, it is important to ask who attends these institutions and why (Aronowitz, 2000). Community colleges are generally the only open-enrollment institutions in higher education, which generally means that they accept any student with a high school diploma or the equivalent. With increasing restrictions being placed on higher education institutions in terms of accepting students who are not proficient in speaking, reading, and writing English, or those who need remedial education, the community college has become the most likely option for many such students. We also know that people of color, those with low socioeconomic status, and many other marginalized students are represented in great numbers at US community colleges (Martinez-Wenzl & Marquez, 2012). These demographics and institutional restrictions, combined with the lower cost of attending community college, have helped to create a type of sorting machine, a process for determining who receives what type of educational opportunity. For institutions, these decisions "depend on whether their clientele is the elite or the plebes, whether they are educating an intellectual leadership, the business class, the political class, or those destined to function in technical categories" (Aronowitz, 2000, p. 5). Given the increasingly hegemonic corporate influence and the culture of technical training associated with the community college curriculum, "opportunity for working-class and minority students is restricted to the skills and dispositions associated with corporate profits" (Ayers et al., 2010, p. 11). As we consider in the next chapter the urban environment, including the right of residents to make and remake the conditions of their daily lives, it will be beneficial to consider the opportunities available to them for obtaining an education and becoming engaged citizens who are able to lead and participate in democratic processes. If we fail to understand the marketing and distribution of these educational opportunities, and to strive to determine how to make them equitable and accessible to all, a moment of possibility and hope may be lost to impact the experience of marginalized urban populations.

At this point, given what we now know of community colleges and the students who attend them, it is appropriate and necessary to step back and observe the coordination and summative effects of several critical and related aspects of these institutions and their students. We understand that the community college curriculum has become increasingly vocationalized in recent decades, now putting greater emphasis on specific technical skills directly related to middle-skilled employment opportunities. We understand that this vocationalization has taken place with less input from faculty curricular experts, with more input from professional administrators, and that such curricular decisions are increasingly influenced by corporate and industry partners, channeled directly, via venture philanthropy, and supported by entities of the state. These curricular changes have created further mission differentiation and stratification among the different segments of higher education. We also understand that there is a sorting of students within higher education, and that students marginalized by class, race, ethnicity, gender status, disability, and other classifications are represented at US community colleges in disproportionate numbers. These students, who already face significant challenges, are further subordinated by being relegated to receiving educational opportunities that are increasingly focused on middle-skilled employment, in contrast to students with different demographic profiles, who benefit from a wide range of opportunities in other segments of higher education. For these students, this constitutes a subalternization in the form of being offered a more limited and different educational opportunity.

We also understand that students from urban environments are more likely to attend community colleges. Subtle but pervasive, the word "urban" itself has been re-codified with changing urban environments, and it therefore has been redefined in how it is used in regard to urban community colleges. Urban existence is often signified by notions of poverty and crime (Anderson, 2013), rather than cosmopolitan sophistication. When we speak of urban community colleges, therefore, the association may engender a perception of the institution as something less than other segments of higher education, and certainly not as an "ivory tower" of possibility, creativity, and critical thought. Serving a higher percentage of students of color and of low socioeconomic status than other segments of higher education, community colleges serve a student population who may be seen as somehow less deserving. As we move forward in this discussion of the role of urban community colleges, it is important to keep the meaning of the word "urban," in both real and perceived terms, at the forefront.

Having offered this investigation into the past and current status of the US community college, including its intimate connection to the economy, I will now address the significance of the changing dynamic in academic decision-making at these institutions by addressing the critical and expanding role they and their faculty play in educating urban populations in the United States. I will do this through a discriminating examination of Lefebvre's conception of a "right to the city," and by scrutinizing the evolution of shared governance in community colleges over the years, shedding light on its nexus with the right to the city. This nexus relies on the foundation of a just education for urban residents, one that will enable them to declare and defend their agency, to think critically, and act to claim their right to speak their word, and in so doing to remake the conditions of their daily lives.

4   A Revival of Lefebvre's Vision of the Right to the City

In this chapter, I explore Henri Lefebvre's notion of the right to the city, a concept originally developed in the turbulent 1960s which has in recent years experienced a revival. This right to the city theory will provide the foundation for my examination of twenty-first-century urban community college students and their ability to determine the conditions of their own lives, the lives of their families and loved ones, and their communities. Using this foundation, I will investigate the connections between community college faculty, students, and curricula, ultimately associating faculty involvement in academic decision-making with an egalitarian education capable of offering deserving students the power and abilities needed for claiming their right to the city.

French philosopher Henri Lefebvre introduced the notion of the right to the city during the revolutionary protests of the late 1960s. The concept focused on redefining the needs and structures of urban life—not only the economic, political, and cultural structures of the city, but also the "social needs inherent to urban society" (Lefebvre, 1996, p. 147). Differentiating from the needs of society related to economic consumption and from the spaces associated with such transactional exchanges, Lefebvre wrote of the complex and contradictory social and anthropological needs the individual has if they are to live a full life in an urban environment, including the need to experience life in all forms, even those not highly valued by policy-makers and city planners. He argued that public spaces where an individual can pursue creative and physical activities, experience art, and simply be able to play are all social needs that are vital to living a rich urban life (Lefebvre, 1996).

These elements of urban living may be studied in what Lefebvre (1996) refers to as the "science of the city," in which the city serves as the object or text of study. Lefebvre's characterization of the city as an object of study is made problematic by his own assessment that the authentic urban environment no longer exists, that it is "falling apart" and "takes the form of a document, or an exhibition, or a museum"—that the city is now "only an object of cultural consumption for tourists" (Lefebvre, 1996, p. 148). He claims that the city as historically constructed is no longer experienced as intended, and, thus, essentially no longer exists as classically perceived. As such, we cannot go back to a now-nonexistent traditional city, nor can we re-create what it was historically intended to be. We can only create a new city "on new foundations, on another scale and in other conditions, in another society" (p. 148).

How can we create a new city in another society? Who would be capable of constructing such a place? Architects, city planners, economists, and politicians would be involved in re-creating the financial, physical, and cultural structures of the urban environment, but they do not have the ability to construct the social relations necessary in Lefebvre's alternate society. Only "social life (praxis) in its global capacity possesses such powers" (Lefebvre, 1996, p. 151). Lefebvre defiantly argues that only "groups, social classes and class fractions capable of revolutionary initiative can take over and realize to fruition solutions to urban problems" (Lefebvre, 1996, p. 154). This revolutionary stance mandates defeating the current dominant ideology and promotes the social and political strategies employed to support such ideology. This process would require both social and political support, which must "depend on the presence and action of the working class, the only one able to put an end to a segregation directed essentially against it" (Lefebvre, 1996, p. 154).

These words suggest that Lefebvre believes that any authentic solution to urban issues, any attempt to remake the conditions of urban living in a new society, must come from within the segregated and oppressed urban working class. This solution has similar parameters to those proposed by Freire (2000, p. 44), who states that it is the "great humanistic and historical task of the oppressed" to liberate themselves, as well as their oppressors, and that in so doing they will restore humanity to both. "Only power that springs from the weakness of the oppressed will be sufficiently strong to free both," Freire adds (2000, p. 44). Furthermore, the oppressors do not have the power to liberate the oppressed; thus, any such effort represents false charity stemming from the perpetuation of an "unjust social order" (Freire, 2000, p. 44). Taken in the context of remaking a new urban societal order, Freire's views support Lefebvre's (1996) claim that the segregated working class must be involved in re-creating an authentic urban social environment capable of sustaining a newly formed society. The presence and action of the working class may not be sufficient to remake urban society, but they are essential to the process. Without their efforts, there can be no progress toward a new city in a new society—and "disintegration will continue under the guise of nostalgia and integration" (Lefebvre, 1996, p. 154).

Writing in 1967, Lefebvre points to a society bent on consumption. He claims that such a society produces a culture dominated by the ideology and rhetoric of positivism, whereby scientific quantification is used to decompose and then redefine urban society to include only the elements of a modern consumptive society. He argues further that such resulting urban societies are devoid of the social and cultural elements that were historically part of the urban environment (Lefebvre, 1996). In this incomplete societal landscape, Lefebvre points to voids that can be filled—what he refers to as "places of the possible"—spaces that "contain the floating and dispersed elements of the possible, but not the power which could assemble them" (Lefebvre, 1996, p. 156). He argues that the power structure of these voids limits the possibilities for these spaces to be realized as a transformative force.

So, while there are spaces of possibility for a new urban social order, and the working class necessary to make these possibilities a reality inhabits such areas, the existing structures of the city fight any such transformation. In this context, the power to make the "conditions of the possible" a reality can only be affected "in the course of a radical metamorphosis" (Lefebvre, 1996, p. 156). This will include a change in technical policy, which must be combined with "social force, capable of investing itself in the urban through a long political experience" (Lefebvre, 1996, p. 156). Only this combination of scientific efficiency and social and political power will produce the type of dialog and social movement necessary to effect change and grant urban residents their right to a renewed and authentic urban life (Lefebvre, 1996).

The ideas behind Lefebvre's seminal work, which introduced the notion of the right to the city, have had a rebirth over the past two decades. The revival and expansion of these ideas have been due less to knowledge of his written work than to the ongoing struggles related to the quality and conditions of everyday urban living, and to the determination of who is able to make and remake these conditions (Harvey, 2012). These efforts have served as the basis for urban social movements around the globe, movements born of longstanding struggles to achieve equity and security related to housing and economic opportunity, and to resolve quality of life issues that plague poor and otherwise marginalized urban populations. As in the time of Lefebvre's original work, current movements associated with social struggle have been significantly influenced by the responses and sensibilities of those immediately impacted by the conditions of urban living (Harvey, 2012). These responses may include "the hopes that lurk as immigrant groups bring life back into a neighborhood" and "the despair that flows from the glum desperation of marginalization, police repressions and idle youth lost in the sheer boredom of increasing unemployment and neglect" (Harvey, 2012, p. xi).

While many leaders of these recent movements had never even heard Lefebvre's name, the urban social struggles in which they were engaged were similar to those which prompted Lefebvre's work, and they led to some of the same conclusions. Fundamental to these conclusions was the belief that the varied struggles of urban populations could and should be coalesced into a collective struggle to claim urban residents' right to make and remake the social conditions of their lives (Harvey, 2012). There have been exceptional examples of such social movements in the global south, notably as expressed in language included in the Brazilian Constitution of 2001 that guaranteed the right to the city. In the United States, inspired by the success of social movements in Brazil, the 2007 US Social Forum held in Atlanta saw the formation of a "Right to the City Alliance," with chapters in various US cities. A consistent feature of most such efforts is that they have risen up from the streets and neighborhoods "as a cry for help and sustenance by oppressed peoples in desperate times" (Harvey, 2012, p. xiii).

Lefebvre's work was a philosophical study of oppressed urban populations. His emphasis on the urban working class as a necessary actor in any radical metamorphosis was a groundbreaking notion for the day, at least in terms of traditional Marxist thinking, which held that the factory worker was the root force of revolutionary change (Harvey, 2012). Believing that revolutionary movements often have an urban component, Lefebvre placed the urban working class at the center of such struggles. In his writings, he noted that the urban working class had different group tendencies than the traditional class of factory workers. He believed that factory workers tended to be settled into steady, long-term positions, whereas the urban working class was more "fragmented and divided, multiple in its aims and needs, more often itinerant, disorganized and fluid" (Harvey, 2012, p. xiii). In this way, Lefebvre's view was inconsistent with leftist thinking of a half century ago, though it now appears to have portended the economic conditions of the twenty-first century. Today, there are fewer full-time employment opportunities available, and fewer stable career paths that offer upward mobility (Aronowitz, 2013). There is still work available, but it is increasingly being done by part-time, itinerant, and contingent workers who have no expectation of receiving health insurance or a pension, or even a commitment from the employer for future work. Changing economic practices and employer attitudes toward full-time employment, combined with advances in technology and the shrinking world associated with an ever more global economy, have led to a radically altered work environment, in addition to the aforementioned reduction in available full-time jobs (Aronowitz, 2013). Even in the field of education, where more full-time career opportunities still exist compared to other fields, the nature of employment is changing dramatically, becoming more fragmented, itinerant, and fluid. For example, in higher education, the large majority of college courses are taught by part-time, contingent faculty who work from course to course for low pay, no benefits, and little to no job security. This is a dramatic change from the past, and there are few signs there will be a major reversal (Aronowitz, 2013).

The changing dynamics of employment, including the decline in full-time career opportunities and the increase of part-time contingent labor, indicates that, if there is to be a radical remaking of the conditions of urban life to include what Lefebvre (1996, p. 156) referred to as the "conditions of the possible," then his vision of the fragmented, itinerant, fluid urban working class as a necessary part of the process must become a reality. In the twenty-first century, this means that part-time workers must be an integral force in any potential right to the city movement. While Marxist and anti-capitalist movements have been gaining momentum in recent years, particularly in the global south (Harvey, 2012), the traditional Marxist vision of the working class must be reconsidered in a twenty-first-century vision of the right to the city. The notion that part-time workers must be engaged in any process of remaking the conditions of urban living is a new dynamic, one that tells of the need for organized movement within a historically unorganized labor force.

When considering the right to the city, it is logical to ask, to whom does the right justly belong? In *Capital,* Marx writes that it is power that decides between multiple claims to a right (Harvey, 2012). In the United States, there is no shortage of examples of cities that have been "remade"—Chicago, Detroit, New Orleans, for instance, and a number of smaller cities—which means they have been gentrified to serve the desires of the local, national, and transnational corporate entities that have power (Lipman, 2011). These various entities represent the power elite, those already in control of remaking urban spaces. Remaking the city through discharge of such power is not an exercise of the right to the city. The right to the city does not belong to those already in power but to the poor, oppressed, and disenfranchised, those who have been left to struggle alone. The right to the city is much more than the right of an individual, a group, or some other entity to claim as their own the resources of the city, such as housing, employment, and public space. It is a collective right to claim "on behalf of the dispossessed their right to the city—their right to change the world, to change life, and to reinvent the city more after their hearts' desire,"—in short, to remake the urban environment into a place where people want to live and grow and perhaps change, remaking themselves as they remake the city (Harvey, 2012, p. 25).

Lefebvre (1996, p. 156) points out that claiming the right to the city requires a "radical metamorphosis" that uses not only technical, scientific policy practices but also social force. This call for revolutionary action has romantic appeal, but it faces daunting odds when that action is to be situated counter to the powerful hegemony forged over time by the corporate elite. For the hopeful revolutionary, this romanticism far too often "crashes against the rock of his [sic] understanding of capitalist realities and capital's power" (Harvey, 2012, p. xvii). There have been outbreaks of revolutionary transformation, a noteworthy example being the Occupy Wall Street movement, but to date none has been sustainable to the point of effecting significant social change. To be successful, movements must be broad and encompass an array of collaborators—true social movements of diverse actors (Harvey, 2012).

There are many reasons why such movements have the potential to claim the right to the city. Some of these arise from capitalist economics, some from race, and a variety from implementation of neoliberal ideology. Such ideology marginalizes specific populations and often reduces the notion of social justice to "access to markets, ignoring differences in access to monetary, legal and social resources" (Hursh & Henderson, 2011, p. 176). Urban policies and planning that involve gentrification often focus on reclaiming urban resources, such as land zoned for public and low-income housing, for development and private wealth accumulation.

Such policies marginalize not only the populations but also the neighborhoods where they live, characterizing certain areas as dangerous, blighted, and in need of being dismantled and re-created to serve a different purpose (Hursh & Henderson, 2011). Those who gain this control take what had been a public good—often land in a prime location—for economic profit and convert it into a private good, such as an economic city center (Lipman, 2011). This loss of land in urban areas also signifies growing racial inequality, as land used for the good of all suddenly becomes a private good for the few, which certainly does not include the oppressed, racially and economically segregated former residents who have been pushed to the outskirts of both the city and society (Lipman, 2011), with the underlying rationalization that any individual who cares to do so may work his or her way to a better future, closer to these new economic and social centers.

Just as land can be privatized as a result of gentrification policies, so too can education. This has been particularly prevalent in public schools serving working-class and poor neighborhoods. Education policies focused on testing, turn-around plans, closing neighborhood schools, and opening more charter schools are taking what was a public good and converting it into a private good (Lipman, 2011). These diverse yet intimately related practices are backed by the highest levels of corporate power and money. In the face of such power, individuals engaged in social movements, including those marginalized by a variety of factors, may feel, and may largely be, powerless to effect changes in the conditions of everyday urban living. They may not even be able to imagine a situation where members of their community gain control over the resources others want to claim in order to accumulate greater wealth. For real change, the oppressed must first be able to conceive of claiming, and then must claim, their right to speak their word (Freire, 2000), to engage in dialog regarding the social circumstances of their community, and act collectively to bring about a radical metamorphosis of the conditions of their living. How this metamorphosis occurs may vary among the different constituencies of the movement, but each constituency plays a critical role in what ultimately must be a collective reclaiming of an "urban commons," a place and space used for the public good.

In addition to the radical metamorphoses needed to change the current conditions of urban living, the impact the present circumstances will have on future populations must be considered. This includes whether future conditions will provide a firm foundation that supports urban dwellers' ability to develop a full, productive, and rewarding life. This will require addressing the heavy-handed elements of education and social policies that have created the current oppressive urban conditions for certain segments of the population. While oppressed individuals may feel powerless to effect change in their own lives, an additional challenge involves considering the social changes necessary to positively impact future generations. This latter necessitates imagining the circumstances which would support a radical metamorphosis not only in order to dynamically change current conditions, but to support change which addresses the controlling relationship between the present and the future, a political movement with a concern for intergenerational justice (Innerarity, 2012). Such a metamorphosis would provide a platform for the future. When considering urban residents' ability to claim their right to the city, it makes sense to also consider the sons and daughters of the victims of "root shock"—those who have been pushed to the outskirts of the city and society. Such victims' offspring will grow up not knowing what it means to have the deep and fertile social grounding that was stripped from their parents. Their social, political, and worldly foundations will be even more fragile than those of the previous generation, and they will have even less authority to control the conditions of their existence.

In order to address such generational issues, social theory must consider the eras of and the interactions between different generations. Social theory often treats different times and generations separately, but "any question about justice between generations must also take into account the fact that the generations interact, that history is not a succession of discontinuities" (Innerarity, 2012, p. 16). There is in fact a close relationship between generations, just as there is between present policy and future consequences. This realization leads to the sobering and problematic conclusion that the short-term vision of present actions may come at the expense of long-term consequences: "The problem with our democracies is that our political antagonisms are bound to the present. We live at the expense of the future; our relationship to it is completely irresponsible" (Innerarity, 2012, p. 3). In financial terms, this includes privileging short-term profits over long-term investments; in social terms, it references a material form of colonialism. Short-term decisions about education policy that focus on short-term employment opportunities for students and short-term profit opportunities for employers are favored over long-term decisions that view education as a form of planning for growth, leadership, and civic responsibility. Innerarity (2012, p. 8) refers to this as the "tyranny of the present." He questions whether today's citizens have more rights than their descendants will—and whether such organized irresponsibility in fact steals from the future. Small doses of this apparent irresponsibility may appear quite reasonable to some, but a coherent and just future will not be the result of an aggregation of short-term and short-sighted decisions. When considering Lefebvre's notion of the right to the city, the rights of future generations must also be considered. The current struggle may focus on an individual's or a collective ability to claim their voice, but, as this liberating process plays out, we must be mindful of protecting the voices and the hope of future generations to claim their rights and responsibilities within a just civil society.

Local Context: New Bedford and Fall River, Massachusetts

While Lefebvre (1996) and Freire (2000) are known for the work they did decades ago in countries other than the United States, Lipman (2011) and Harvey (2012) are more contemporary; while all four examined different cities in different generations, the concepts of their work transcend time and location. The textual materials of this particular study are varied in both geographic and generational origin. As such, the framework for this study is descriptive of many urban areas, including where this research project was undertaken. The University of Massachusetts Dartmouth, where I engaged in this work, is located in southeastern Massachusetts on Buzzard's Bay, an area known as the South Coast. It sits between the urban centers of New Bedford and Fall River. I have lived in this area for most of my adult life and have been employed by Bristol Community College, which has a campus in both of these cities, for more than two decades. During the time I engaged in the work which led to this book, and perhaps more importantly, during the many years prior as I lived, worked, and explored ideas of faculty voice and community college education, my geographic frame of reference was this area.

Located just fifteen miles apart, New Bedford and Fall River are both relatively small; New Bedford has a population of over 95,000, and Fall River 89,000 (US Census, 2018). These two urban centers represent one of the most economically and educationally depressed regions in the state. The per-capita income for both cities is just over $21,000, less than 60 percent of the state average of almost \$36,000. More than 23 percent of both cities' residents live in poverty, more than twice the statewide rate, and the numbers are worse for children under the age of eighteen—34 percent in New Bedford and 36 percent in Fall River, also more than twice the statewide rate (SCUIP, 2016). As might be expected in an economically depressed area, measures of educational attainment also fall on the low end of statewide figures. In both New Bedford and Fall River, almost 30 percent of adult residents have no high school diploma, 61 percent have never earned any college credits, and less than 15 percent have earned a bachelor's degree or higher. This low level of adult educational attainment is reproduced in the New Bedford and Fall River public school systems, where four-year high school graduation rates are 61 percent for New Bedford and 68 percent for Fall River, both significantly below the statewide rate of 86 percent (SCUIP, 2016). It is important to point out that these numbers, which give a sense of the challenges faced by New Bedford and Fall River, only represent the current circumstances, which have been molded and reproduced by multiple factors. Every locality is of course impacted by social, political, and economic factors as diverse as the community itself, and this is no different for New Bedford and Fall River. The current demographic measures reflect complex communities with social, labor, and cultural histories that today are largely invisible. These many real and impactful socio-historical factors—which are reproduced in current school, housing, and civic policy—are easy to overlook and too easily erased from official knowledge. Thus, local context will remain central to any interpretations in this study, including any consideration of a student's claim of their right to the city.

Given the proximity of the University of Massachusetts Dartmouth and Bristol Community College to these two cities, as well as my longtime residence and employment in the region, the economic and educational circumstances of the residents of New Bedford and Fall River were a motivating factor for this study. New Bedford and Fall River are former mill cities with proud histories and residents who exhibit a strong work ethic. Both cities have experienced a transformation in the labor market similar to that in many other US cities, as steady long-term mill and factory work has dissipated into more fragmented part-time work (SCUIP, 2016). This transformation has brought the New Bedford and Fall River workforces into closer alignment with Lefebvre's notion of the fragmented and divided urban working class. This transformation to a new economy, combined with low levels of educational attainment, has helped to cement the status of these two cities as centers of low economic opportunity and low educational achievement, which has in turn led, for residents, to high levels of poverty and membership in an oppressed population. A half a century after Lefebvre's groundbreaking work, the cities of New Bedford and Fall River offer a clear and current example of residents marginalized by economic and educational circumstances. Like so many urban populations around the globe, many of the cities' residents have struggled to achieve equity and security around a variety of quality of life issues. The environmental conditions in which many residents of New Bedford and Fall River live have dictated the conditions of their existence. This situation offers an environment ripe for a revival of Lefebvre's vision, but as with other urban centers in other context, to revive the vision of the right to the city, residents must be prepared with the necessary skills, attributes, and abilities to speak their word and claim their right to make and remake the conditions of their lives.

The Right to the City: A Role for Community College Faculty

Education must be an essential element of right to the city movements. Any such movement must create alliances among a diverse array of social interest groups, just as any social movement in education should build alliances with—and value the input and perspectives of—a variety of community members, including teachers, students, parents, and others who are invested in creating a vibrant education system for the community (Lipman, 2011). These alliances are vitally important in education today, due to the growing impact of neoliberal ideology and the associated privatization of what have historically been elements of the public sphere.

In particular, teachers are critically important in any such movement. Movements which focus on the public sphere, those impacting collective elements and members of society, including public schooling, are often concerned with issues of social justice. According to Weiner (2012), teachers are "idea workers" who, ideally, foster the autonomous and critical modes of thinking that lead students to consider ideas related to freedom, equality, and social justice. While to the corporate elite, teachers may be considered "dangerous," due to their role "equipping students with skills, competences, abilities, knowledge, and the attitudes and personal qualities that can be expressed and expended in the capitalist labor process"

(Hill & Kumar, 2012, p. 19), to others they are idea workers concerned with their students. Such concern for social justice and the public good counters much of the market-driven activity of recent decades in which goods such as public housing and public schooling have increasingly been privatized. There is hope, however, that a transformative education can become a tool for liberation in some of the most oppressed communities in the United States. These communities are largely segregated by race and class, and many of them have been targeted for gentrification, pushing already marginalized residents not only to the outskirts of society but to the outskirts of cultural and economic opportunity (Lipman, 2011).

In the battle in recent decades to privatize spaces for the public good, significant efforts have been launched to silence student, parent, teacher, and community voices and critiques in the elementary and secondary education systems. These increasingly successful efforts to replace public oversight of schooling with private have been partly supported by the complicity of teachers and their unions (Weiner, 2012). By focusing only on the elements of education that impact teaching conditions, salaries, and benefits, some teachers and their unions have ignored vitally important alliances with community partners. Many union members and union leaders have underestimated and underutilized the power of collective membership and institutional strength, and in so doing have abandoned one of their greatest assets in combating the neoliberal assault on public education (Weiner, 2012). For those who work in a unionized environment, and who aim to effectively support public interests, this collective power may be claimed by teachers who believe that "the union" is not simply a set of elected officers/representatives, but rather that it is a collective effort of all members who individually see themselves as an integral part of that effort. This collective power must then be used to advocate on behalf of students, teachers, parents, and the community (Weiner, 2012). Also critical is the notion that, in a social movement, the power does not come from one source: community alliances, including recognition and support for others' interests and recognition of common interests, can be a critical source of support. Therefore, the teacher/faculty member has a significant role to play in a right to the city movement.

This work has discussed at length the changing conditions of US cities, the higher education system, and the role of US community colleges. We recognize that there is a significant population of urban residents, often those who are marginalized and oppressed and segregated by race and class, for whom the very conditions of their existence have been under attack for the purposes of profiteering and wealth accumulation by corporate entities. To remake the conditions of their daily existence in the face of such opposing forces, these populations must claim their right to speak their word, and then use this right to promote a radical metamorphosis and create conditions that are capable of sustaining meaningful change. In order for residents to reinvent the city in a way that reflects their own desires, the power of the movement must come from the streets and neighborhoods and be supported by democratic processes and authentic community leaders. Education must play a key role in creating such community leaders. Plagued by current neoliberal policies that focus on high-stakes testing, turn-around plans, school closings, and privatization, America's cities have public education systems that have largely been stripped of the creative and critical tools that can help them develop such community leaders—leaders who are prepared to question the conditions of their existence and work to effect transformative changes for themselves, their families, and their communities. Given the existing public education and social policies applied to this initial deficit condition, providing access to higher learning becomes paramount.

This study has demonstrated that the only path to higher education for many marginalized urban residents is the community college. It has also shown that community college faculty and curricula have been impacted by vocational corporate interests more than other segments of higher education. These two facts point to the unavoidable conclusion that many marginalized urban students, who are often segregated by class and race, are being guided toward a different type of education—one more likely to have a focus on short-term employment skills—than students with the means and ability to attend a baccalaureate-granting institution. This reality seriously hinders the urban population's ability to grow leaders and to remake the conditions of their daily living, and thereby to claim their right to the city. This condition lays bare a fundamental structural inequity of the US higher education system, one that may only be overcome through transformative leadership and critical change.

If we believe that poor and otherwise marginalized urban college students should not be directed toward vocational programs that provide short-term employment skills more than other college students, and that curriculum decisions should be placed in the hands of the curricular experts rather than professional managers and corporate interests, then community college leaders need to know that, for the sake of students and their communities, faculty need to be re-engaged in academic governance and curricular decisions. The existing hegemony of professional management is so strong that doing this will likely require another sort of radical metamorphosis, but it is nonetheless a critical step. The transfer of decision-making power from faculty to professional administrators has been so complete that many do not understand that faculty held that power not so long ago. Those who do understand that historical precedent may have become too cynical or downtrodden to act, a degree of demoralization that translates "less into moral outrage than into cynicism, accommodation, and a retreat into a sterile form of professionalism" (H. A. Giroux, 2014a, p. 17).

This hegemonic control and suppression of many higher education faculty members make it even more important to examine the faculty-student relationship as a space of higher learning and critical thought. Aronowitz (2000) states that the main function of faculty is not teaching but "providing an intellectual environment that will encourage the learner to dispense with intellectual authorities and to become her own authority" (p. 143). Faculty must now perform this liberating act for themselves and create an environment in which they dispense with managerial authority and reclaim their own. This will be no easy task, particularly for community college faculty, most of whom are part-time employees, a group that is "fragmented and divided, multiple in its aims and needs, more often itinerant, disorganized and fluid" (Harvey, 2012, p. xiii)—characteristics similar to Lefebvre's description of the oppressed and marginalized urban working class. Even full-time faculty have some of these characteristics, as they increasingly accept academic decisions and industry-driven curriculum justified by a lack of resources, management prerogative, and students' desire for an education that prepares them for employment. If faculty members are to achieve a radical metamorphosis, they must do so with a liberating praxis, "the action and reflection of men and women upon their world in order to transform it" (Freire, 2000, p. 79). To do this, they must claim their right to "speak their word" (p. 88) and must use this right to engage in dialog regarding academic decisions, the rationale for such decisions, and the impact such decisions have on students. No one else can do this; they must do it for themselves.

There are many ways for the community college faculty member, whether full-time or part-time, to engage in this critical dialog, although none may be as effective as an organized faculty movement based in local leadership and organization. Many community colleges already have organized faculty unions that can be used to conduct this dialog. Institutions without a faculty union may have a faculty senate or other autonomous faculty organization created by like-minded faculty leaders interested in creating dialog and transforming institutional culture and practice, and where a similar process may be fostered. No matter what the name of the organization, it must be constituted by a collective and democratic organization of faculty.

Established unions at many institutions follow a business model, with a primary focus on faculty salaries, benefits, and working conditions. They may have little faculty involvement beyond a few elected officers (Weiner, 2012), and in such cases, this lack of democratic and broad faculty involvement should be addressed. Dialog regarding faculty engagement in decision-making is still possible in such cases, but it will require a transformation of organizational structure and priorities to include a broader array of faculty interests, including the administrative decision-making process. Even a small number of like-minded faculty interested in regaining decision-making authority can begin a dialog within such a faculty organization, which may lead more individuals to claim their voice and, ultimately, to a transformation of institutional structures. This process will take leadership and organization and will likely require the liberation and transformation of the faculty organization in order to achieve the liberation and transformation of the institutional governance structure. The faculty organization must be a democratic space of collective faculty voice that supports dialog, caring, and the ability to support movements that empower faculty to effect institutional and social transformation.

For the many reasons outlined above, faculty should strive to control the academic program at all community colleges, reclaiming the right to develop and teach a curriculum that provides students with more than the short-term technical knowledge needed to gain immediate employment. Community college students deserve and need the critical thinking skills often found in a liberal arts curriculum, as well as the tools to theorize and analyze political structures of power and social resistance (K. Saltman, personal communication, March 6, 2015). They need the skills to interpret, transform, and adapt to an ever-changing global world and, further, to become autonomous, self-directed learners. These are the skills truly desired by employers (Nussbaum, 2010), and the skills future urban leaders will need to control the conditions of their lives.

To make such an education more available to community college students, faculty must claim and invest in their stakeholder rights within existing institutional parameters, while working to expand such rights. Community colleges have various formal levels of faculty involvement in governance, but, whatever the level, faculty should engage in governance processes to the greatest extent possible. This statement must be accompanied by an acknowledgement of the varied ability of faculty to engage in institutional processes, based on their varied conditions of professional and personal existence, including the conditions of part-time, contingent faculty, working for low pay, with no benefits or job security, and at multiple institutions. Even with this recognition, the level of engagement and the processes for faculty to engage in governance can be discussed and negotiated with faculty and administration, through a faculty or academic senate, collective bargaining union, or through an autonomous group of concerned faculty members. Two essential principles to strive for in any such work related to faculty organization should be (1) to ensure transparency in academic decisions made at the institution and (2) to ensure that the faculty voice is heard in these decisions. Institutions that operate by these principles will have taken a foundational step toward returning academic decision-making to the curricular experts, and restoring public and democratic oversight to institutional governance. How a faculty group secures these integral principles may depend on institutional circumstances and climate, but success will be more likely and more lasting if any such structured faculty movement utilizes the collective strength of the faculty by using public and transparent processes in which many faculty participate and all faculty have the opportunity to be included. If efforts to work collaboratively with college administration do not look promising, a faculty group may take a more unilateral approach to creating dialog, such as a research project culminating in a public white paper. Such a project would likely be a last-ditch effort to foster dialog between faculty and the administration, but it could be a powerful tool in opening a dialog.

No matter the form or process used, such a dialog may challenge and embolden faculty to exercise their collective and autonomous voices in support of institutional change. There are many challenges, institutional and structural, to engaging in this dialog. There are also personal challenges, including claiming faculty voice by many harried community college faculty at the helm of transformation efforts, who may have been excluded by institutional processes and the hegemony of current neoliberal norms. By claiming their voice, engaging in dialog, and creating institutional structures which value faculty voice, faculty have the unique opportunity to address the very real social, economic, and personal needs of their students. This includes providing for their students an education which supports not only the skills and abilities to succeed economically, but also to develop as engaged members and leaders of their communities, while creating a space and opportunity for authentic social transformation.

In summing up the connection between education and social transformation, Aronowitz (2000) asserts that possibilities for "genuine social and cultural as much as scientific innovation depend, not on following others, but on the formation of an autonomous self capable of finding its own voice" (p. 144). It is precisely the fostering of this autonomous self that is needed to create new urban leaders and actors in our cities. The social, cultural, and political conditions of recent decades have failed urban populations and those who might otherwise have striven to remake those conditions. Failed by policy, public education as a mode of reproduction has failed these populations. For millions of urban residents, the local community college provides their only opportunity to receive an education that will enable them to grow into autonomous leaders capable of remaking the conditions of their existence. Much as the marginalized urban resident must claim their voice in an effort to remake the conditions of their daily environment, so too must the marginalized community college faculty member claim their voice in an effort to remake their professional lives and the conditions of educational opportunity.

5 On Recognition and Redistribution

In this chapter, we will investigate the relationship between the historic shift away from community college faculty being recognized as curricular and governance leaders, and the potential for redistribution of decision-making power toward faculty. To do this, we will first examine Nancy Fraser's (2000) rethinking of historic efforts to recognize differences in cultural identities of minority and underrepresented groups, and how such efforts have impacted the struggle to redistribute power and wealth to these groups, and then make a parallel argument related to community college faculty. To do this, we will investigate Fraser's (2000) argument that, while promoting the recognition of cultural identities of populations has directly neither helped nor hurt efforts to redistribute power and wealth, in effect, identity recognition efforts have markedly displaced redistribution efforts. This result, which may be unexpected to many, has been further complicated by the reification of efforts to recognize group differences, as recognizing the cultural identity of one group may alienate them from other groups, which can lead to anger and bigotry based on group differences. Fraser's (2000) rethinking of the recognition and redistribution dynamic offers a redesigned recognition model that supports redistribution efforts. Instead of focusing on the cultural group identity, her model focuses on the individual. She specifically proposes that every individual must be recognized as a full and valued participant in the social interactions of life.

Building on Fraser's model, I will argue that involving community college faculty in academic decision-making is a form of status recognition. Recognizing the individual faculty member as a full partner in the social interactions that determine academic decisions is more important than the group faculty identity—anything less represents social subordination. I also reference Fraser's (2008) later work, which further rethinks recognition and redistribution, arguing that the best solutions for redistributing wealth and power can coexist with a recognition of group differences. I use this work to argue for a transformative approach to engaging community college faculty in decision-making, one that blurs the line of cultural recognition between faculty and administration. Finally, I argue that recognizing the status of community college faculty will promote a more just and democratic society, as it will help to create a broad, inclusive curriculum based on an ecology of knowledges (Sousa Santos, 2014).

The 1970s and 1980s saw many cultural struggles, often emancipatory in nature, calling for the recognition of differences, including those of race, ethnicity, gender, and sexuality. These were battles not only for recognition of denied cultural and human identities but also for redistribution of wealth and power. By the turn of the twenty-first century, recognition of differences had intensified and become part of a global discourse that included such issues as national sovereignty, multiculturalism, and human rights (Fraser, 2000). As identity recognition increased, there was a simultaneous and antithetical decline in the call for the redistribution of wealth and power. This decline coincided with the rise and increased dominance of a neoliberal ideology, which assailed the egalitarianism of a Keynesian social welfare state and called instead for a form of social Darwinism that holds firm to the neoliberal tenet of individual responsibility above all else (Fraser, 2000).

This move toward a recognition of differences and away from the redistribution of wealth and power has had significant consequences. First is the manner in which such struggles have manifested. Today, globalization's faster and more intense intercultural interaction, communication, and migration are making the world a smaller place. This situation is exacerbated by an ever-present and intrusive global media, which makes the manifestation of cultural recognition more problematic. Such systematic assertions related to cultural differences, including claims of recognition made more conspicuous and public by the mechanisms of globalization, have also exacerbated cultural intolerance (Fraser, 2000). What may be seen by some as a show of respect and recognition for one cultural group may in reality foster resentment and bigotry in others, who view themselves as having their own social recognition and economic issues. With cultural recognition efforts ever more present due to instantaneous and insidious global communication and interaction, such efforts may make others perceive inequality and tyranny in their own life circumstances, further intensifying the neoliberal focus on the individual, while eschewing concern for the social well-being of others. As a result of this conflict and heightened intolerance, many have relinquished their struggle for cultural recognition and assimilated into the cultural prescription of the dominant class (Fraser, 2000).

A closely related consequence of moving toward recognition of cultural identities has occurred in conjunction with economic globalization and the aggressive expansion of capitalism, which have intensified economic inequality (Fraser, 2000) and further increased efforts to gain recognition of group identities. This increased focus on recognition of cultural differences has not had a positive effect, as one may have presumed, on the redistribution of wealth and power. In fact, coupled with manifestations of bigotry, the impact has been negative, if indirect, in that efforts to focus on group identities, while not directly impacting redistribution efforts, have in effect displaced the focus on redistribution of wealth and power in many populations. The result is that cultural group identity recognition thus has served to "marginalize, eclipse, and displace" redistribution efforts (Fraser, 2000, p. 108).

Fraser (2000) proposes that the way to solve such issues is by reshaping the concept of recognition so it can coexist with efforts to redistribute wealth and power. She argues that a new conception must be created that encompasses the intricacies of cultural recognition while mitigating the problems of reification, including the propensity in recent decades to foster intolerance and separatism. To do this, Fraser counters Hegel's identity model of recognition with a model based on the recognition of status.

Hegel's identity model treats individuals as equal and separate subjects; each individual recognizes the other, which leads to a sense of self (Fraser, 2000). The problem occurs when an individual is denied recognition or is misrecognized, leading to their being devalued by the other and by the dominant culture. This often results in a poor self-image and a lack of cultural identity for the one who has been denied. This Hegelian view of identity states that those who are denied recognition, or who are misrecognized, must contest this disparagement and help to create a self-affirming culture that will enable them to gain the respect of the dominant culture (Fraser, 2000). However, focusing solely on recognition of cultural identities is problematic, as it does not address how the reification of cultural identities leads to intolerance and separatism. Also missing in this analysis is how treating recognition independently from issues of distribution ignores those of social injustice. By ignoring the impact of the unjust distribution of wealth and power, recognition and identity politics can supplant redistribution as a potent cultural force (Fraser, 2000). Linking cultural norms to economic forces seriously erodes the socioeconomic foundation for the denial of recognition, and of misrecognition. Assuming conditions of inequitable economic distribution, focusing solely on cultural identity ignores the privilege of those who benefit from a concrete support structure and have fewer barriers to success. These barriers may be political and social as well as economic, thus exacerbating the boundary between recognition and misrecognition—or they may constitute a complete denial of recognition (Fraser, 2000).

There are those who recognize and want to remedy inequitable economic distribution while also believing that distribution issues are a result of improper recognition. From this perspective, a society that can advance recognition will see a positive impact on economic distribution. However, this view increases the problems of displacement by focusing solely on the recognition of cultural identity, even with redistribution as its stated end (Fraser, 2000).

The Hegelian view of identity stresses that those who are denied recognition or are misrecognized must contest this false characterization, and in so doing create a self-affirming culture that will gain the respect of the dominant culture (Fraser, 2000). Fraser contends that the pressure of identity politics fosters resignation and thus assimilation to certain cultural norms. In this climate, cultural dissent and experimentation are shunned, and identity politics all too often distills down to a single, conventional group identity. This recursive process establishes yet again the problems of the reification of identity, including a rejection of critique and dissenting views, the stultifying claim to the authenticity of the dominant norm, and a continuing opportunity for intolerance and separatism to play a dominant and suppressive role in cultural circumstances (Fraser, 2000).

As a counter to the Hegelian identity model, Fraser (2000) proposes that recognition be considered a matter of social status:

> From this perspective, what requires recognition is not group-specific identity but the status of individual group members as full partners in social interaction. Misrecognition, accordingly, does not mean the depreciation and deformation of group identity, but social subordination—in the sense of being prevented from participating as a peer in social life.
>
> (p. 113)

The status model proposes that subordination may be overcome by confirming the misrecognized individual as a fully participating member of society, whose status is equal to all other members. Absent that equality, the social construct is defined by institutional and cultural factors that distinguish some as representing the norm while relegating others to an inferior class. This form of misrecognition is a type of institutional subordination, one that denies not only status but equality and recognition as a fully participating member of society. It is not based in cultural identity but in "institutionalized patterns of cultural value that constitute one as comparatively unworthy of respect or esteem" (Fraser, 2000, p. 114). This institutional subordination is unjust, and there is no simple remedy. Each institutional and cultural circumstance may dictate a different solution, and each solution must address institutionalized structures and patterns of cultural value in order to remove barriers to equal participation. This means changing the values that govern institutional activity, no matter the circumstance. Therefore, any viable solution must be accepted in institutional culture, and must seek "to overcome status subordination by changing the values that regulate interaction, entrenching new value patterns that will promote parity of participation in social life" (p. 116).

The status model of recognition is impacted by factors other than institutionalized patterns of cultural values. Maldistribution of resources may limit the ability of some members of a society to participate as cultural peers, as well as their ability to claim equal status. The status model of recognition thus acknowledges that recognition and the distribution of resources are intricately related (Fraser, 2000). The model recognizes that status is related to institutionally defined cultural values and societal parameters, but it also allows critique of—and connection to—the distributive elements of society. Such a critique inevitably includes considerations of socioeconomic class, including the distribution and maldistribution of wealth and power. Such considerations are often ignored in societies dominated by neoliberal ideology, which hold that wealth, poverty, and power cannot be used to explain or excuse issues related to cultural and social reproduction. Fraser (2000) ignores this dominant ideology and positions the status model of recognition squarely within the overarching socioeconomic foundation. In so doing, she interrelates the critical elements of the status model, defining each as an element of subordination, the subordination of not being recognized as a full-participant in institutional culture, as discussed above, and the distributive subordination of increased economic inequality. While neither injustice is completely reducible to or overcome by the other, this framework has enabled Fraser (2000) to establish a theoretical solution that rethinks and reforms a concept of recognition that coexists with the realities of economic distribution and mitigates both the displacement of redistribution by identity recognition and the problems of the reification of cultural identities.

Faculty Commitment as a Matter of Recognition and Redistribution

Parallel to the cultural struggles for the recognition of differences and redistribution of wealth and power of the pre-neoliberal era, the rapid expansion of community colleges in the 1950s and 1960s played an emancipatory role for a growing population of Americans. Supporting the vision of President Truman's 1947 Commission on Higher Education, community colleges were seen as a compelling public good, a mechanism to enhance both the wealth and the life circumstances of students, and a means of supporting a free and democratic society (Schrum, 2007). In this way, these institutions offered liberating public support for both personal and public objectives. By the turn of the twenty-first century, recognition of both cultural identity and the need for higher education had intensified. During this time, the need for community colleges was affirmed, with an associated increase in enrollments, but there was a simultaneous and antithetical decline in the decision-making power of community college faculty. As shown earlier, this coincided with the growing dominance of neoliberal ideology and of higher education governance structures that increasingly mimicked market-based business principles.

The increased recognition of community colleges' importance in serving a diverse and growing student population, coupled with faculty's declining role in academic governance, has had two significant consequences. First, these changes occurred in a time of dramatic advances in technology, competition, and economic globalization, when the need to increase the availability of higher education to more citizens was complicated by competition to provide such services. This competition occurred in an environment further confounded by the associated loss of geographic boundaries made possible by dramatic advances in technology, including the ability to communicate globally and the capacity to instantaneously share information. With the recognition that higher education must be accessible to more of the populace, the community college faculty's loss of power has largely been ignored. It has been displaced by the importance of the community college and the social and economic benefits it provides members of the community who find themselves in ever more challenging circumstances. In this way, the displacement of redistribution efforts by identity politics is thus mirrored in the similar displacement of community college faculty voice by claims of the importance to student-life enhancement. Many view the benefits of a community college education as liberating. Recognition of this purpose is a powerful tool, one that is supported by faculty, though this faculty support assists in further entrenching the hegemonic nature and condition of community college governance. The inclination to consider the importance of faculty in such work has declined, thereby ceding the work that so critically defines the direction and purpose of these institutions to the forces of technology, competition, and non-academic professional management. In this way, the recognized importance of the community college has in fact facilitated the marginalization and displacement of faculty in matters of institutional governance.

A second consequence of the acknowledged importance of community colleges in the US higher education system is the manifestation of their standing and the associated transformation and expansion. As discussed in Chapter 3, as early as the mid-twentieth century, community colleges were known as nimble institutions capable of adjusting rapidly to market and governmental needs. With technological advances and increasing globalization, this institutional ability has been further enhanced. With the declining funding for public higher education in the neoliberal era, community colleges have also increasingly been transformed by their need to generate independent revenue sources. The need to be entrepreneurial in order to ensure financial survival has forced the community college to increasingly adopt business model practices, more closely aligning the institutional ethos of the community college with the goals of production, efficiency, and solvency. Furthermore, government classification of community colleges as centers for workforce education and training has placed increased pressure on management to operate in a fiscally responsible manner, and to align the institution's direction and curriculum with corporate economic purposes.

These factors have successfully classified community colleges as economic institutions, and are a major result of the taken-for-granted recognition of their prominence in the realm of higher education. This phenomenon has become ever more problematic, as managerial aspiration has become less encumbered by faculty engagement in academic decision-making. The determination of institutional operation and focus is largely assigned to professional managers who are often far removed from—or have never engaged in—academic work at the leading edge of inquiry, instruction, and the creation of knowledge. The result is that academic decisions are commonly made by managers who lack the requisite academic expertise. In this environment, community colleges are increasingly recognized for their key role in educating American students, a recognition that brings a subtle, unspoken, hegemonic exacerbation of educational intolerance and inequality along cultural and socioeconomic lines. What many see as open access to educational opportunity may in reality be an opportunity to engage with a curriculum intended for a specific economic purpose, which provides an altogether different social experience. It is critical that an education engenders respect and recognition while avoiding unequal opportunity. This is more and more difficult to do in an education system which is increasingly fashioned by other than a faculty governance model. In a system permeated with a market ethos and dominated by a neoliberal ideology, one where recognition of community colleges manifests in a current-day assimilation to an economic model that fosters a relinquishment of faculty engagement, it is faculty's fundamental right and responsibility to be engaged and to ensure economic, as well as educational and cultural, equality for the students and communities they serve.

In the course of this work, I have addressed problems related to the community college faculty's displacement from academic decision-making, and the reification of recognition of the community college as an essential element in the current higher education system. Applying Fraser's (2000) concept of recognition and redistribution, any solution for these problems must involve a rethinking and reforming of the concept of recognition in a way that coexists with efforts to reengage faculty in academic decision-making, and, in so doing, helps to redistribute the power of institutional governance. To do this, any new conception must encompass the intricacies of community college culture, while at the same time mitigating the hegemonic problems of reification. This includes fostering cultural respect for and acceptance of community colleges and their purposes, while recognizing the unique challenges they face in serving their students and communities, such as the pervasive reliance on part-time, contingent faculty. Only then can we recognize the status of community college faculty, while examining and addressing the contradictory yet vital role they play in addressing, as opposed to exacerbating, educational intolerance and inequality along cultural and socioeconomic lines.

In this regard, failure to link the norms of US community colleges to the inequitable distribution of decision-making power only strengthens the foundation of not only the current misrecognition of community colleges as spaces solely for economic development but the failure to recognize these institutions as spaces of higher learning that are capable of transforming lives and developing capable community leaders.

This issue is critical in addressing the reification of the community college identity within the larger structure of higher education. Identity politics in the dominant culture promote a broader cultural withdrawal from responsibility and resignation that the cultural norm of the community college is solely an economic rather than a social engine. In this milieu, educational experimentation and diversion from the dominant view of the community college as a center for economic generation are discouraged. The result is a notion of the American community college that has been distilled down to the lowest common denominator of educational purpose, a purpose that promotes economic activity over the social or cultural. In this environment, educational activity that supports short-term economic development for individuals and businesses is privileged. Lost in this newly refined identity is any notion of support for society and culture that is not expressed in economic terms. Lost is the former foundational purpose of higher education as supporting democracy and democratic institutions. What remains is a narrow economic functionality disguised as higher learning. This notion of education results in an educational model that is devoid of potential for critique and originality, and it lacks the curricular purpose of impacting communities by developing socially engaged citizens and leaders who are able to transform the conditions of their daily existence and of their communities.

Recognition of the community college identity has not redistributed decision-making power to the faculty. In fact, this identity recognition has helped to displace any redistribution to the effect that faculty now wield even less decision-making power. This issue may be redressed by a recognition not of the community college group identity or even of community college faculty, but by considering Fraser's (2000) notion of recognition as a matter of social status. Applying Fraser's model, what must be recognized is the status of individual community college faculty members as full participants in the academic decision-making processes. Lack of recognition or a misrecognition of this status is not an attack on the identity of community colleges or their faculty but an act of civil subordination, one that suppresses faculty members and declares them to be something less than peers, and deprives them of being full partners in the actions and interactions that define and form academic decisions. Such subordination includes both a lack of inclusion of the faculty member and a lack of transparency and openness by those, likely professional managers, who do have such civil status.

If a faculty member's status has been denied or they have been misrecognized, this subordination may be overcome by the individual being institutionally validated as a full participant in the interactions that define institutional governance processes. In other words, a denial of recognition or a misrecognition of status can be remedied. Each case of institutional subordination constitutes a unique injustice based in the cultural circumstances of that particular community college and that particular instance. As such, there is no one solution for all cases; however, each must redress the structures and institutional values that create barriers to faculty members' full participation. Each instance of subordination for which no remedy is found presents a social construct defined by institutional and cultural factors. This grants some faculty members a status that allows them to engage in academic governance but withholds such status/engagement from others. Those denied such status are relegated to a subordinate and inferior class, and are denied the respect and value of being recognized as fully participating members of the academic community and the institution.

The concept of recognizing the status of community college faculty rethinks and reforms the notion of recognition and the connection between recognition and redistribution. In the status model, recognition complements and coexists with the redistribution of academic decision-making power to faculty members. Unlike the identity model, the status model does not engage a larger group identity, and thus reification is not an impediment. Moreover, a recognition of status does not displace redistribution efforts, but instead illuminates institutional structures and values that impede full faculty participation in academic governance. Fundamental to the status model is the critical concept that recognition is associated with each individual faculty member. Considering the faculty member's social status within the institution allows the identification of the specific characteristics of the social subordination and local circumstances that describe the lack of faculty involvement in governance in every unique instance. Therefore, if there is to be a remedy for the social subordination of faculty, the processes associated with a recognition of status in a given/particular context will help to identify that remedy.

In the years following Fraser's (2000) groundbreaking work on rethinking recognition, she continued to engage with the subject of the displacement of socioeconomic redistribution by cultural recognition. In her later work, Fraser (2008) reconsidered the recognition-redistribution dilemma, searching only for remedies that supported measures of cultural recognition that could coexist with a politics of equality and social justice. Framing the dialog in this manner, she examined ways that economic disadvantage and cultural disrespect not only coexist but in fact support each other. Reframing the recognition-redistribution dilemma as cultural injustice versus socioeconomic injustice, Fraser searched for coinciding solutions to such struggles. While distinct, such injustices are usually interrelated and reinforce one another:

> Cultural norms that are unfairly biased against some are institutionalized in the state and the economy; meanwhile, economic disadvantage impedes equal participation in the making of culture, in public spheres and in everyday life. The result is often a vicious circle of cultural and economic subordination.
>
> (p. 16)

As issues of injustice may reinforce one another, a remedy for one injustice may conflict with a remedy for another. Claims of cultural recognition often promote social group differentiation, while claims of socioeconomic redistribution are likely to "promote group de-differentiation. The upshot is that the politics of recognition and the politics of redistribution appear to have mutually contradictory aims" (Fraser, 2008, p. 18). Two types of remedies may be used to frame a potential solution: affirmative remedies, which aim to address "inequitable outcomes of social arrangements without disturbing the underlying framework that generates them," and transformative remedies, which address "inequitable outcomes precisely by restructuring the underlying generative framework" (Fraser, 2008, p. 28).

Whether dealing with remedies for purely economic redistribution efforts or for the redistribution of academic decision-making power among community college faculty and professional administrators, affirmative remedies redress end-state maldistribution but do not disturb the underlying power structure that reproduces the injustice. Such affirmative redistribution efforts produce change on the surface but not the kind of structural change that will impact future injustice. Affirmative remedies for cultural recognition similarly reallocate cultural respect, but do so only on a superficial level (Fraser, 2008). In contrast, transformative remedies for redistribution—whether of economic power or of academic decision-making power—constitute a deep restructuring of power relations. They blur the lines between cultural groups, thus helping to address mutual misrecognition. Furthermore, transformative remedies for cultural recognition offer a profound deconstruction and reconstruction of social constructs. While affirmative remedies do have benefits, they tend to reaffirm structural elements that lead to further injustice in both redistribution and recognition efforts. Transformative remedies, including claiming community college faculty participation in academic governance as a matter of recognition and redistribution, hold more promise. Such efforts have the most potential to blur the lines of class differentiation within the community college, which would also blur the line between the professional administrator and the faculty administrator while reestablishing deep faculty engagement in academic decision-making.

The Privilege of Knowledge

In the arguments made so far, we have considered the tenets of neoliberal ideology and their associated impact over the past four decades. We have paid particular attention to the impact this ideology has had on higher education, above all to the ways faculty have been marginalized in influencing academic decision-making at colleges and universities. We have situated the last four decades of community college reforms within the dominant neoliberal framework and considered the role these institutions have played in educating urban populations, particularly in terms of urban residents claiming their right to the city. We also have examined the function of community college faculty and claimed their role in academic decision-making as a matter of recognition and redistribution. However, if we are to provide a successful remedy for the recognition of faculty as vibrant and essential contributors to the process of community college governance, then we must consider the endgame of this process, as well as the curricula and forms of knowledge that will be privileged in what we propose. Our aim is that these efforts will produce an egalitarian education able to develop urban leaders. If we propose to provide students with an education that will promote their "primordial right to speak their word" and engage in dialog "mediated by the world, in order to name the world" (Freire, 2000, p. 88)—an education that leads to self-liberation and gives urban residents the ability to claim their right to the city—then we must ask what vital components academic faculty as decision-makers will contribute. We recognize that faculty are at the forefront of educational activity, including instruction, inquiry, and the production of knowledge, but we also must consider the question of epistemic privilege and ask what/which/whose knowledge is to be produced/shared/consumed.

The right to the city, which enables individuals and communities to make and remake the conditions of their daily lives, is a response to the social injustice that occurs in urban areas across the United States. Sousa Santos (2014) situates social injustice more broadly, since "Ultimately, social injustice is based on cognitive injustice. However, the struggle for cognitive justice will never succeed if it is based only on the idea of a more equitable distribution of scientific knowledge" (Sousa Santos, 2014, p. 189). As discussed previously, the scientific positivism of the current global hegemonic pedagogy has been imposed as the dominant element of today's higher education curriculum. This government- and corporation-supported curriculum has been infused throughout higher education, though we have discovered that particular emphasis has been placed on technical and scientific knowledge that supports workforce education and training at community colleges. This can be particularly troubling when considering the critical role community colleges play in educating urban populations. In his seminal work introducing the notion of the right to the city, Lefebvre (1996) notes that a focus on quantification and scientific knowledge ultimately disintegrates urban culture, and then redefines it to include only elements of a modern consumer society. This process re-creates a sterile urban environment devoid of precisely the elements that have historically defined the city's social and cultural life. When one claims their right to the city, they are seeking exactly these lost elements of authentic social and cultural urban life, which are so vital to the process of remaking the conditions of urban existence. In these circumstances, and with the community colleges' crucial role in urban education, these institutions must cultivate the conditions for authentic personal and communal renewal. Community colleges must offer a broad curriculum that includes science and technology among many subjects, and that supports multiple perspectives and cultures, not just the dominant culture. Introducing what he calls an "ecology of knowledges," Sousa Santos (2014, p. 42) calls for "an intercultural dialog and translation among different critical knowledges and practices: South-centric and North-centric, popular and scientific, religious and secular, female and male, urban and rural, and so forth." This intercultural dialog is at the heart of the ecology of knowledges, and is precisely what the educational processes of an urban education need to support urban residents' right to the city.

The road ahead for community colleges is not an easy one, and there is no single recipe for success. My claim is that by recognizing the status of faculty as fully engaged participants in institutional governance, these institutions, with their faculty, may begin the process of examining the logic and education that we value. Through this process, we will discover a route that makes sense for our locality and the students we serve, even if it does not conform to our own knowledge or that of the dominant culture. Moreover, we must consider that the monoculture of scientific knowledge presented to us by the dominant culture may not be the only route. We must critique and challenge this culture by offering other knowledges and associated alternate criteria for assessment of rigor, including consideration of knowledges that may exist and thrive in subaltern cultures. We may identify epistemologies previously relegated to extinction or perhaps those yet to be conceived. Within this realm of infinite knowledge, we must understand that "the impossibility of grasping the infinite epistemological diversity of the world does not release us from trying to know it; on the contrary, it demands that we do" (Sousa Santos, 2014, p. 111). Sousa Santos calls this imperative the "ecology of knowledges," and within this climate of exploration lies the possibility of a liberating education, one worthy of personal and communal reclamation. It is here that we find the basis of the intellectual and cultural knowledge needed for a truly liberating and egalitarian education. We find the knowledge learned individuals need, no matter their history or the history of their culture, to understand themselves and their lives in the context of their environs and the world. This broad, critical, and inclusive basis of education allows the individual to critique the unknown and allows community leaders to critique the conditions of their existence and the greater society. It also enables them to consider ways of knowing previously unconsidered in their social realms and how those ways may influence and galvanize their lives and the lives of others. This type of educational exploration allows individuals to critique the efficacy and relevance of the knowledge on which their education is based, and also to question the hegemonic authority claimed by the dominant culture in creating educational policy and curriculum.

The ecology of knowledges also has a place for ignorance of knowledge, which allows one to unlearn or ignore knowledge that is disqualified by new learning. New learning is critical to a foundational principle of the ecology of knowledges, "equality of opportunity" (Sousa Santos, 2014, p. 190), which demands that all knowledges have an equal opportunity to impact individuals and the larger society. This equal opportunity of knowledge provides an egalitarian epistemological foundation that respects and privileges difference, and leads to both a more intense democracy and a more just society. The prospects for social justice are intimately connected to those opportunities for cognitive justice, which are a consequence of the ecology of knowledges. Within a diverse and ever-changing epistemological foundation, we find the nexus of an education that can create the conditions in which an urban community college student can discover the intimate relationship between their educational experience, their personal experiences, and the communal opportunities presented to them and their families. In these circumstances, propelled by an education that supports self- and communal-liberation—one fashioned by educators who espouse a curriculum worthy of an ecology of knowledges—the community college student has the opportunity to impact not only their own development but that of their community. Buoyed by knowledge of themselves, their culture and society, and of other knowledges, the student can claim their right to speak their word, engage in dialog, reflect and act on their world, and, in so doing, to make and remake the conditions of their daily existence while claiming their right to the city.

Of course, this is all very difficult to achieve within the current hegemony of American higher education, and even more so in the directed community college system. If we are to create change that fosters a more just and egalitarian community college experience, particularly for poor and otherwise marginalized urban students, I argue that we must be sure that faculty are recognized as fully participating members of the institution's academic decision-making culture. We have outlined the conditions of this metamorphosis, which relies unequivocally on community college faculty gaining their right to speak their word and to liberate themselves from their current status of having been misrecognized or denied recognition altogether. Since many faculty have been relegated to a subordinate and inferior class within the institutional academic decision-making apparatus, their role in the governance process has been effectively colonized.

To overcome the current hegemony of community college governance structures, which has become ever-more dominant in the years since the dawn of neoliberal higher education policy, these institutions must decolonize their current governance structures and the role the faculty plays within them. The possibility of such a transformation for community college faculty has been, in effect, rendered less likely, as neoliberal ideology has vilified many things which in the past were seen as part of the public good, including public service workers such as community college faculty, public spaces, and public education. All the while, recognition for these workers and their work has become more uncertain, as the changing conception of public education and educators has brought a changing perception of community college faculty. As public workers have come to be seen as a drain on tax revenues and as cogs in the workforce training apparatus of public education, recognition of faculty as integral to the operation and management of community colleges has waned. With this loss of recognition has come an associated lack of respect. Community college faculty are misrecognized by many, including by those who do not recognize or value investment in the public good. By some, they may even be perceived as lazy state workers with high salaries, short work hours, exorbitant benefits packages, and all at taxpayers' expense. Faculty have and must continue to fight any such lack of recognition and misrecognition. Though, any fight for recognition has seemingly been displaced by a diminishing hope of regaining their former position as respected full partners in the social interactions that constitute the governance of their institutions. All of this makes the subordinate role of faculty in decision-making much more of a problem in need of a remedy.

The decolonization of subordinated cultures, particularly those of developing non-Western cultures, has been widespread over the past half century. Concrete and visible steps have been taken within these cultures, many of them manifested in liberating political and policy changes, but for colonization to be truly transformed at its roots, there must also be a psychological element to decolonization. One example is illustrated by Aristides Pereira, the first president of Cape Verde after that country gained independence from Portugal.

In one of his speeches as President, Pereira pronounced, "We made our liberation and we drove out the colonizers. Now we need to decolonize our minds" (Macedo, 2009, p. 124). In the process of liberating itself from colonial rule, Cape Verde was able to unite in its understanding and internalization of the fact that the country's reliance on Portugal was a false reality. This psychological decolonization is key to unity since, as Freire (2000) writes,

> In order for the oppressed to unite, they must first cut the umbilical cord of magic and myth which binds them to the world of oppression; the unity which links them to each other must be of a different nature.
>
> (p. 175)

For Cape Verdeans, achieving this unity required an awareness that any perception of an umbilical cord connecting Cape Verde to Portugal was a false construct, a connection manufactured by Portugal in the interest of maintaining control during colonial rule. Liberating itself from its subordinate status, Cape Verde and its residents "cut the false umbilical cord . . . For there to be a real umbilical cord there had to be an existential-historical connection, and in the case of Cape Verde there was none" (Macedo, 2009, p. 123).

A parallel argument may be made in the case of community college faculty and their engagement in academic governance. The unity that links faculty to each other must have at its core a common recognition of faculty as full participants in academic governance, accompanied by a decolonization of the mind. Community college faculty too often accept that professional managers make academic decisions with little or no faculty input. There are varied degrees of acceptance that the faculty role in governance is first as implementer, second as recommender, and third as administrator/decision-maker—if faculty are at all involved in this realm. Acceptance of professional management of and faculty marginalization from academic governance must be severed not only from practice but from subjective reality. The existential-historical connection must be revealed to be that of the faculty-administrator, and not faculty's current disconnection and insulation from administrative governance. As Cape Verde did after cutting the false umbilical cord with Portugal, faculty will have to learn to accept and live in a different reality, one where they not only are identified as vibrant and essential members of the decision-making stratum, but where they also understand and identify their own status as part of that stratum. Community colleges, as represented by both their administrations and their faculties, must work to decolonize the minds of all personnel as well as institutional processes, thereby allowing a counterhegemonic liberation not only for faculty but also for administrators and other professional staff. Only by so doing will community college faculty be fully able to claim their right to speak their word and engage in dialog that may provide an alternative to the current hegemonic reality.

Conclusion

This study has a deeply critical ideological foundation, one that demands that public policy be intimately connected to the personal and civil elements of society. This foundation makes undeniable connections between social and political policy and critical elements of social theory. My position is in part the result of my upbringing, and, taken by itself, may seem to be pure common sense. However, in this book I have laid bare the contradictions of the current political reality. Due to these factors, my ideological view of the world and my analysis of the work of many critical theorists, my research, and the resulting interpretation must all be understood as elements of an inherently critical study, one that connects policy to social circumstances as a matter of course. I have drawn on the varied spheres of activity and analyses of some of the leading public critical intellectuals and educators within and beyond Western epistemological platforms, while conducting my investigations from the same critical ideological stance. On this foundation, I have laid out a theoretical framework that has led this study to certain undeniable conclusions. These conclusions connect and relate elements of my framework, and demonstrate that the framework itself is an integral part of the study design, one that has allowed the object of study to be examined in carefully interrelated terrains.

Vitally important to this work are the characteristics of community college students. Community colleges educate more urban students, first-generation college students, and students marginalized by factors such as race, ethnicity, class, and gender than other segments of higher education. While the primary focus of this study is the erosion of faculty voice in community college academic decision-making, its critical nature calls for a consideration of the social impact of this loss of voice—the impact on community college curriculum and on the education offered to community college students. Community college education is intimately connected to the way students interact with and function in society; therefore, the circumstances of the community college student are not only a motivation for this research study but a foundational component of the arguments made and the conclusions drawn.

This book considered as discourse is a profoundly social exercise. The conversation begins with the voice of faculty in academic decision-making and concludes with the associated impact on the social lives of students. The research framework has guided the reader along a series of epistemological avenues that have intimately connected the voice of the faculty to the life of the student. While it is understood that this research framework is immersed in a critical social ideological milieu, it is nonetheless an appropriate environment for studying one of the most social of the sciences—education.

Over the past four decades, the forces of market ideology have caused the state to abandon public services and responsibilities in favor of creating markets that privatize and claim significant elements of the public realm for private profit. This marketization of public entities has been accompanied by an undermining suspicion of majority rule and the democratic principles and processes that are the foundation of the United States. In recent years, political and legal processes have been sold to the highest bidder. A virtual state of exception in the force of law allows private entities to skirt legal and civil constraints in the name of wealth accumulation. Public protections have been conveniently ignored in the name of private and corporate control of systems originally created for public good. The tool of debt has been used to shackle individuals, institutions, and (formerly) sovereign political entities to a state of servitude to private capital. The financialization of every aspect of society has become a fiscal act of language, a promise to repay. No longer is commercialization based solely on an economy of goods and services. Across the globe, and certainly in the United States, the political and ideological project of neoliberalism has reduced human and social interaction to that of a financial interaction; human interaction as a therapeutic measure is now ignored. The control and alignment of the social elements of society with the financial have become so ingrained and accepted, so completely infused in the hegemonic way of life in the United States, that we do not even question private capital's control of formerly sovereign political entities. In this environment, it is accepted as the norm that public institutions are and should be economic institutions that support private enterprise and markets.

This study has demonstrated that the market ethos of neoliberalism and the installation of an associated political project over the last four decades have had a dramatic impact on higher education in the United States. The once proudly and nationally articulated mission of public higher education—to provide an education in support of a free and democratic society as a social and public good—is now little more than a quaint notion of a time gone by. In an era when private corporate money is not only allowed but invited, even encouraged, to create markets in order to profit from public goods and services such as education, a free and democratic society is a near impossibility. The dominance of private capital over public policy has been shown to defeat the democratic purposes of public higher education. Market ideals incorporated into both policy and practice have decreased the emphasis on free thinking and critique as essential elements of public higher education. These elements, which should be the fundamental ingredients of higher learning and must be supported by strong academic freedom for faculty and the general understanding that higher education is and should be a public good, are among the elements of policy and practice that have been under attack in recent decades.

Given that higher education has mimicked the corporate model—including college presidents being referred to as CEOs, critical elements of public institutions and services being privatized, and increased emphasis on education and training as an economic good, along with a decreasing emphasis on inquiry and critique as a social good—this study has shined a spotlight on the role of faculty in that corporate context. The role of faculty in shared governance and the historic role of the faculty administrator have been dramatically affected throughout all of higher education. These roles are now largely filled by professional administrators who may or may not have come through the faculty ranks. Moreover, professional administrators who are former faculty rarely return to the faculty role and a professional life of teaching and scholarship. They tend to retreat from academic life as the years pass, becoming less and less connected to their subject area expertise. Administrators who are less connected to academic subject areas than current faculty nevertheless wield great power in setting academic and curriculum policy. They often are considered, by themselves and others, to be managers rather than academics doing managerial work. In recent decades, during this process of transformation, there has been a tremendous shift in the balance of power away from faculty and toward professional administrators. Moreover, these managers may be concerned with moving up the educational corporate ladder, which leads to the fundamental problem that some individuals in administration positions—who are determining the direction and actions of educational institutions—may be more concerned with their own ambitions than with serving their students' aims or with the needs of students' families and communities. This type of ambition may guide individuals to make administrative decisions based on personal advancement rather than institutional and student interests. Even if rare, this influence of neoliberal ideology is as illustrative as it is harmful. It identifies the educational work environment as a marketplace that assigns value to individual advancement of the professional administrator over the historic and correct purpose of higher education—the success of the students and the impact their success has on their families and communities.

There is another significant factor impacting academic decision-making. As higher education institutions further mimic the business model, corporate partnerships with these institutions continue to become more intricate and intense. Partnerships and shared resources lead to some individuals serving as trustees on both corporate and educational boards, further blurring the line between private and public purpose. Private funding of research and academic programming at public institutions and support of programs geared toward specific industries can lead to financial ties that may impact institutional decisions. These decisions may be academic, and as such represent yet another influence on the erosion of faculty voice in the academic decision-making process. Moreover, the dominance of private capital over public policy influences higher education funding streams in profound ways, including policy leading to the defunding of public higher education by the state, and the resulting normalization of venture philanthropy as an accepted funding stream, replete with ideological conditions attached. Such private influence over the revenue streams of public higher education further separates these institutions from the public realm.

If the primary purpose of higher education is to be recognized as supporting a free and democratic society, if it is ever again to serve as an incubator for civic leaders who can transform society in ways that serve the public good, we must consider what colleges and universities should be doing. We must understand the current hegemony of public higher education policy and have the courage, foresight, and stamina to address its damaging elements, those that privilege private over public good and individual over societal concerns. It is only in so doing that we may return the right of public education to the care of the public.

It is important to point out that not all community colleges are the same; their faculties have differing degrees of involvement in academic decision-making. Indeed, with well over one thousand community colleges across the United States, it should be expected that some institutions have managed to keep the oppression of market ideology at bay. There are wonderful examples of faculty engagement in shared governance, and of deep, critical, and civil engagement in their school's social order. It also should be expected that there are excellent examples of community colleges with curricula that foster students' ability to claim their right to the city. But in the main, this study has shown that neoliberal market ideology has had a manifestly negative effect on American community colleges and the students they serve. This ideology, which has advanced the entrepreneurial freedom of the individual over the collective rights of society, has not only had a grossly impugning effect on the individual citizen but an adverse effect on community colleges—the very institutions that serve some of the most marginalized and forgotten college students in the country.

When considering the condition of American community colleges, their administrations, faculty, and the students they serve, we may start with a more general conversation about the state of higher education in the United States. Community colleges are a subset of this discussion, as they have been impacted by the same forces. As described in Chapter 3, they have also been subject to a variety of forces unique among higher education institutions. For more than a century, they functioned as junior college transfer institutions, educating students who went on to study at baccalaureate granting colleges and universities. Community colleges also have proudly served the purposes espoused by the Truman Commission, wherein public higher education is a compelling public good that contributes to the common well-being by preparing citizens to participate in activity that helps to maintain a free and democratic society. Community colleges have also proven to be flexible institutions, able to adapt quickly to serve a variety of purposes, including the development of new academic programs in short order. While this characteristic may often be beneficial, as when providing a service to the local community that other, more rigid institutions might not be able to offer, the malleability of the community college also calls for caution. The ability to retool and change so quickly makes the community college a prime target for abuse by corporate interests, as these institutions are able to adapt to new and ever-changing technological advances and changes in industry more quickly than other institutions. They can immediately adjust the curriculum and thus quickly and readily impact the education afforded the community college student.

While this study has shown that the vocationalization of the curriculum has occurred at all levels of higher education, the extent to which community colleges and their students have been singled out for technical education targeted at specific employment opportunities is unique. The technical skills needed for these jobs are desired by employers, and, in the hegemonic connection between education and employment, many students, parents, and educators see this link as quite appropriate. However, there are multiple problems with this development. The technological nature of employment is changing so rapidly that many employees need to retool their skillset on a somewhat regular basis. Along with the loss of the critical thinking and communication skills that occurs in an education focused on specific technical training, we see that students directed toward these programs are offered a different type of educational opportunity than students at other institutions. These differing opportunities lead to fundamental social, political, and ethical considerations insofar as we must determine the essential elements students who attend community colleges need to gain from their education. Further, we must examine the conditions that can—or cannot—provide this type of education. Such considerations are the foundational motivation for this study.

This study has demonstrated that neoliberal education policies have had a dramatic negative impact on the public schooling afforded children in poor urban neighborhoods. These policies have significantly contributed to gentrification efforts that push the most oppressed populations to the outskirts of the city and of society. These populations, often already marginalized by poor schools, root shock, and economic blight, live with limited economic and educational hope. For those in such neighborhoods across the country who do successfully navigate the school system and earn a high school degree, who return to school to earn a high school equivalency certificate, or who study to gain proficiency in English, community colleges can play a vital role in providing postsecondary education. The community college is in fact frequently the student's best—or indeed only—viable option.

Since they are significant foundational element of the research framework for this study and resulting book, it is critically important to closely scrutinize urban community college students and their ability to claim their right to the city. This ability relies on students having not only the raw materials to make and remake the conditions of their daily existence but also their having the power to assemble those materials and fully claim their right. In his seminal 1967 work, Lefebvre referred to voids in the lives of urban residents as "places of the possible [that] contain the floating and dispersed elements of the possible, but not the power which could assemble them" (Lefebvre, 1996, p. 156). The urban community college student has the floating and dispersed elements, the talent and intellectual ability, the materials needed to claim their right to the city and to define the conditions of their life. What they may lack in this space is the force to transform their locality into a space of empowerment and liberation. They may lack the power to coalesce the elements of their life and, in so doing, to spark a radical metamorphosis, one that has the power to define and shape their community and their life to be worthy of their aspirations and respectful of what they long for.

A half century after Lefebvre wrote of these voids in the lives of urban residents and the transformative power needed to convert them into "places of the possible," his work remains an appropriate and necessary lens through which to view urban environments. It also was a powerful motivational force for this research study. The same voids exist today in oppressive urban cultures dominated by financial rather than human models of social interaction. Perhaps more than ever, the hegemony of today's unfettered free market ideology has hidden any sign of liberating power. There is hope for a redeeming education for urban community college students, but only to the extent that it is built on a solid foundation of education existing in a social context, one connected to the particular lives and aspirations of those students. An education primarily focused on learning specific technical skills for a particular job or field cannot possibly integrate the elements of the lives of urban students, will not foster the necessary radical metamorphoses, and will not cultivate the reflective leadership skills community college students need to claim their right to the city. In a right to the city movement, what is needed is an education that promotes the development of social and political skills that are vital for community engagement and supporting democratic ideals.

If we believe that, in the current environment, an on-ramp to educational opportunity is key to helping urban community college students claim their right to the city, and that the community college curriculum offered these students is a different, more vocationally oriented educational opportunity than that offered students at other types of institutions, then we must put a halt to community college policy that is based on market ideology. If we believe that a faculty voice in academic decision-making is critically important to the type of education these students receive, then we must identify strategies to reinstitute that voice in order to promote a curriculum that supports students' ability to claim their right to the city. Furthermore, if we want the community college student to have a revolutionary impact on their own lives and communities, and if we believe faculty engagement in academic and curricular matters is of paramount importance to their doing so, then we must chart a course that enables community college faculty to themselves experience a liberating reclamation of their voice. As discussed in Chapter 4, community college faculty have experienced a degree of oppression at the hands of neoliberal forces and policies. But just as faculty strive to foster in their students the ability to dispense with authority and to gain their own agency, they themselves do not necessarily follow their own advice, advice which would be in both their own interest and that of their students. In the process of self-liberation, faculty must work to achieve a radical metamorphosis of their own. They must gain their own voice and use it to speak their word.

If education is to play a role in the community college student's ability to claim their right to the city, then community college faculty must take an integral role in the process. It is not the goal or the right of this treatise to provide a recipe or roadmap for faculty to follow to remedy the current circumstances, as such a prescribed remedy is almost sure to fail. This discourse, engaging various critical views and works, written in a particular locality, and examined from a singular perspective, has offered a number of avenues that may hold promise. For example, it has suggested, and the author strongly believes, that organized faculty movements such as senates and social movement unions are vitally important in connecting faculty to social and community organizations, enabling them to garner strength and support from individuals and organizations with common interests. The collective strength of such organizational movements will empower faculty not only to liberate themselves but also to liberate a limited vocational curriculum from the forces of neoliberal hegemony and policy. This study also espouses the vital conclusion that, no matter the collective recognition of group identity, in order to achieve redistribution of decision-making power in higher education, and in order for faculty to reclaim their position as the essential creators of a curriculum worthy of student liberation and leadership, each individual must be recognized as a full partner in the academic decision-making strata of their institution. Such broad-based power and agency are essential to moving forward, and crucial to the faculty, the curriculum, and the students they serve.

Although the mission of the American community college has morphed over the past several decades, a relatively constant element has been that these institutions play an integral role in providing an education for those who want to enter the workforce in any number of industries. Employment in these industries has been dynamic, largely due to fast-changing technologies. This has created a higher education system composed of layered strata, with a different mission at each layer. The goal of this project is not to make a monolith of the varying strata or to turn every community college into a liberal arts institution that grants associate degrees, but to lay bare some obvious and contradictory truths about the American educational system. In the vocationalized environment of the US community college system, some of the most oppressed college students in our country have been set up with an education that is unworthy of the important and lofty, yet reasonable, goals they have for themselves, their families, and their communities. Students marginalized by a variety of factors have been sold a bill of goods in thinking that higher education equates to gaining specific employment skills for the ever-changing technological economy. Indeed, a primary lie of the current-day hegemony of neoliberalism is that education equates to training for employment. This ignores one of the most fundamental principles set forth by John Dewey a century ago, namely, that education must be intrinsically connected to the social environment and that this connection is a foundation of American democracy. Dewey also recognized that work is an intrinsically social activity and is intimately related to society. However, an education based primarily on providing the technical skills needed for specific employment does not make the critical connection between education, work, and the social life of the student and community. As such, it is not an education that will create a civically and socially engaged citizen.

As I have argued throughout this work, public policy must be interwoven with the personal and civil spheres; faculty voice can and should play a fundamental role in ensuring that these important connections stay robust and locally relevant. Our students, our faculty, our institutions of higher learning, and our democratic society have been betrayed by the oppressive hegemonic corporate influences in current education policy. This policy is deeply ingrained in our community college system and in the curriculum, and it is increasingly accepted as the unquestioned truth by students, educators, and society. The current circumstances have been defined within a confining, neoliberal environment that can only be transformed by a liberating praxis that provides an education worthy of the social and democratic ideals that are the very foundation of our country and in desperate need of revival. This study has suggested that such a liberating praxis can and must come from our faculty, but that any such salvation is only possible if they claim their voice—an emancipating voice of praxis and a voice intimately engaged in the academic operation of their institutions. Faculty must claim and demand recognition of their status as full and essential partners in the academic decision-making process. It is only in this way that they may provide for their students a liberating education worthy of their right to the city.

References

Agamben, G. (2005). *State of exception*. 2003. Trans. Kevin Attell. Chicago: University of Chicago Press.

Anderson, E. (2013). *Streetwise: Race, class, and change in an urban community*. Chicago: University of Chicago Press.

Anderson, G. L. (1998). Toward authentic participation: Deconstructing the discourses of participatory reforms in education. *American Educational Research Journal, 35*(4), 571–603.

Apple, M. W. (1979). *Ideology and curriculum*. London: Routledge.

Aronowitz, S. (2000). *The knowledge factory: Dismantling the corporate university and creating true higher learning*. Boston: Beacon Press.

Aronowitz, S. (2013, October). *Education in a jobless economy*. Department of Educational Leadership Colloquium conducted at the University of Massachusetts Dartmouth, North Dartmouth, MA.

Ayers, D. F., Wilson, D. M., Beaky, L. A., Pohl, R. J., Jenkins, R., Jensen, B., & Newfield, C. (2010). Putting the community back into the college. *Academe, 96*(3), 9–11.

Ball, S. J. (2007). *Education plc: Understanding private sector participation in public sector education*. London: Routledge.

Bauman, Z. (1998). *Globalization: The human consequences*. New York: Columbia University Press.

Berardi, F. (2012). *The uprising: On poetry and finance*. Cambridge: MIT Press.

Bowen, W. G., & Tobin, E. M. (2015). *Locus of authority: The evolution of faculty roles in the governance of higher education*. Princeton: Princeton University Press.

Boyd, S. H. (2011). The spread of neoliberalism in US community colleges: TQM accreditation, "consumers," and corporate sponsored non-profits. *Journal for Critical Education Policy Studies, 9*(1), 242–266.

Brunton, J. E. (2016). VTDigger. *Jennifer Brunton: To the CCV administration*. Retrieved November, 2018 from: https://vtdigger.org/2016/10/20/jennifer-brunton-ccv-administration/

Center for the Study of Education Policy. (2015). Grapevine, Illinois State University. Retrieved May, 2015 from: http://education.illinoisstate.edu/grapevine/

Clarke, J., & Newman, J. (1997). *The managerial state: Power, politics and ideology in the remaking of social welfare.* London: Sage.

Clerkin, K., & Simon, Y. (2014). College for America: Student-centered, competency-based education. *Change: The Magazine of Higher Learning, 46*(6), 6–13.

Couturier, L. K. (2005). The unspoken is being undone: The market's impact on higher education's public purpose. *New Directions for Higher Education, 129,* 85–100.

Davies, W. (2011). The political economy of unhappiness. *New Left Review, 71,* 65–80.

Denzin, N. K., & Lincoln, Y. S. (2000). *Handbook of qualitative research.* Thousand Oaks: Sage.

Dewey, J. (2004). *Democracy and education.* Mineola: Dover Publications.

Dewey, J., & Dewey, E. (1915). *Schools of to-morrow.* New York: E. P. Dutton & Company.

Espino, M. M., Vega, I. I., Rendón, L. I., Ranero, J. J., & Muniz, M. M. (2012). The process of reflexión in bridging testimonios across lived experience. *Equity & Excellence in Education, 45*(3), 444–459.

Foucault, M., & Pearson, J. (2001). *Fearless speech.* Los Angeles: Semiotext(e).

Fraser, N. (2000). Rethinking recognition. *New Left Review, 3,* 107–120.

Fraser, N. (2008). From redistribution to recognition? Dilemmas of justice in a "Postsocialist" age. In K. Olson (Ed.), *Adding insult to injury: Nancy Fraser debates her critics* (pp. 11–41). New York: Verso.

Freire, P. (2000). *Pedagogy of the oppressed.* New York: Continuum International Publishing Group.

Gandin, L. A., & Apple, M. W. (2002). Thin versus thick democracy in education: Porto Alegre and the creation of alternatives to neoliberalism. *International Studies in Sociology of Education, 12*(2), 99–116.

Ginsberg, B. (2011). *The fall of the faculty: The rise of the all-administrative university and why it matters.* New York: Oxford University Press.

Giroux, H. A. (2007). *The university in chains: Confronting the military-industrial-academic complex.* Boulder: Paradigm Publishers.

Giroux, H. A. (2011). *On critical pedagogy.* New York: Continuum International Publishing Group.

Giroux, H. A. (2014a). *Neoliberalism's war on higher education.* Chicago: Haymarket Books.

Giroux, H. A. (2014b, April). *Where is the outrage: Defending higher education in the age of casino capitalism.* Department of Educational Leadership Colloquium conducted at the University of Massachusetts Dartmouth, North Dartmouth, MA.

Giroux, S. S. (2014, April). *On the role of intellectuals in the post-civil rights university: Some DuBoisian reflections.* Department of Educational Leadership Colloquium conducted at the University of Massachusetts Dartmouth, North Dartmouth, MA.

Harvey, D. (2005). *A brief history of neoliberalism*. Oxford: Oxford University Press.

Harvey, D. (2012). *Rebel cities: From the right to the city to the urban revolution*. London: Verso.

Hill, D., & Kumar, R. (2012). Neoliberalism and its impacts. In *Global neoliberalism and education and its consequences* (pp. 32–49). New York: Routledge.

Hursh, D. W., & Henderson, J. A. (2011). Contesting global neoliberalism and creating alternative futures. *Discourse: Studies in the Cultural Politics of Education, 32*(2), 171–185.

Innerarity, D. (2012). *The future and its enemies: In defense of political hope*. Stanford: Stanford University Press.

Jacobs, J. (2012). The essential role of community colleges in rebuilding the nation's communities and economies. In J. E. Lane & D. B. Johnstone (Eds.), *Universities and colleges as economic drivers: Measuring higher education's role in economic development* (pp. 191–203). Albany: SUNY Press.

Jenkins, R., & Jensen, B. (2010). How to climb down from top-down leadership. *Academe, 96*(3), 24–27.

Klein-Collins, R. (2013, November). Sharpening our focus on learning: The rise of competency-based approaches to degree completion. *National institute for learning outcomes assessment*. Retrieved February, 2020 from: https://www.learningoutcomesassessment.org/documents/Occasional%20Paper%2020.pdf

Laclau, E. (2005). Populism: What's in a name?. In F. Panizza (Ed.), *Populism and the mirror of democracy* (pp. 38–48). London: Verso.

Lazzarato, M. (2012). *The making of the indebted man: An essay on the neoliberal condition*. Trans. Joshua David Jordan. New York: Semiotext(e).

Lefebvre, H. (1996). *Writings on cities* (Vol. 63, No. 2). Oxford: Blackwell.

Levin, J. S., Kater, S. T., & Wagoner, R. L. (2006). *Community college faculty: At work in the new economy*. New York: Palgrave Macmillan.

Lewis, A. H. (1963). *The day they shook the plum tree*. New York: Bantam Books.

Lipman, P. (2011). *The new political economy of urban education: Neoliberalism, race, and the right to the city*. New York: Routledge.

Lynch, K. (2014). New managerialism: The impact on education. *Concept, 5*(3), 11.

Macedo, D. (2009). *Literacies of power: Expanded edition what Americans are not allowed to know*. Boulder: Westview Press.

Martinez-Wenzl, M., & Marquez, R. (2012). Unrealized promises: Unequal access, affordability, and excellence at community colleges in Southern California. Retrieved April, 2016 from: http://escholarship.org/uc/item/23c5m52j

Marx, K., & Bender, F. L. (Ed.). (2013). *The communist manifesto*. New York: W. W. Norton & Company

Nussbaum, M. C. (1998). *Cultivating humanity.* Cambridge: Harvard University Press.

Nussbaum, M. C. (2010). *Not for profit: Why democracy needs the humanities.* Princeton: Princeton University Press.

Ortega, J. (1944). *Mission of the university.* Princeton: Princeton University Press.

Paraskeva, J. M. (2007). Kidnapping public schooling: Perversion and normalization of the discursive bases within the epicenter of New Right educational policies. *Policy Futures in Education, 5*(2), 137–159.

Sahlberg, P. (2011). *Finnish lessons.* New York: Teachers College Press.

Saltman, K. J. (2010). *The gift of education: Public education and venture philanthropy.* New York: Palgrave Macmillan.

Saltman, K. J. (2012). *The failure of corporate school reform.* Boulder: Paradigm Publishers.

Schrum, E. (2007). Establishing a democratic religion: Metaphysics and democracy in the debates over the president's commission on higher education. *History of Education Quarterly, 47*(3), 277–301.

SCUIP. (2016). SouthCoast Urban Indicators Project, Public Policy Center of the University of Massachusetts Dartmouth. Retrieved February, 2016 from: http://southcoastindicators.org/

Slaughter, S., & Rhoades, G. (2004). *Academic capitalism and the new economy: Markets, state, and higher education.* Baltimore: The Johns Hopkins University Press.

Somers, M. R., & Block, F. (2005). From poverty to perversity: Ideas, markets, and institutions over 200 years of welfare debate. *American Sociological Review, 70*(2), 260–287.

Sousa Santos, B. (2014). *Epistemologies of the south: Justice against epistemicide.* Boulder: Paradigm Publishers.

Spielbauer, G. W. (2010). America's community colleges: The first century. *ATEA Journal, 38,* 27.

Stiglitz, J. E. (2015). *Rewriting the rules of the American economy: An agenda for growth and shared prosperity.* New York: W. W. Norton & Company.

Tollefson, T. A., Garrett, R. L., & Ingram, W. G. (1999). *Fifty state systems of community colleges.* Johnson City: The Overmountain Press.

Tinberg, N., Richardson, J. T., Burgan, M., Sufka, K. J., Gasman, M., Frew, J., & Cornelius-White, J. (2009). A call for faculty reengagement in governance. *Academe, 95*(6), 8–10.

US Census. (2018). United States Census Bureau. Retrieved February, 2020 from: https://www.census.gov/quickfacts/MA

Veblen, T. (1918). *The higher learning in America: A memorandum on the conduct of universities by business men.* New York: B. W. Huebsch.

Ward, C. V. (2001). A lesson from the British polytechnics for American community colleges. *Community College Review, 29*(2), 1–17.

Weiner, L. (2012). *The future of our schools: Teachers unions and social justice.* Chicago: Haymarket Books.

White House Website. (2014). Retrieved April, 2014 from: http://www. whitehouse.gov/issues/education/

Wilson, D. M. (2010). The casualties of the twenty-first-century community college. *Academe, 96*(3), 12–18.

Wolf, N. (2007). *The end of America: Letter of warning to a young patriot.* White River Junction: Chelsea Green Publishing.

Young, J. R. (2016). MIT dean takes leave to start new university without lectures or classrooms. *Chronicle of Higher Education.* Retrieved February, 2016 from: http://chronicle.com/article/MIT-Dean-Takes-Leave-to-Start/235121

Index